THE LANGUAGES OF
LIGHT

A Creative Approach to Residential Lighting

Artifice
books on architecture

Dedicated to Zach, Honor and Alexander,
the Light of our Lives.

Understanding Light

Even a room which must be dark needs at least a crack of light to know how dark it is.

Louis Kahn

Light in all its magnificent and technicolour glory informs our world. From dawn to dusk the sensational play of the sun creates theatre by manipulating our senses, stimulating our responses and shaping our perception of space. Traditionally we danced to the rhythm of the sun and the soft embrace of the moon. It is this cyclical pattern, created millennia ago, that we respond to both physically and emotionally.

Our use of language highlights these unconscious responses attributing strength and visibility to this invisible medium. Light-hearted, light of my life, drawn to the light—the poetry! Light plays a dominant role in our perception of people and spaces, as we might describe them as bright or enlightened or by contrast dark and shady. Our intuition is often reasoned through the assimilation of 'light' in language.

As lighting designers, we look to the sun, one of our most valuable resources as the perfect source of light. Sunlight, variable in tone and intensity is the tool that transforms our lives. By embracing current knowledge and new technologies we are able to re-establish its power over our well-being and as the foundation for lighting design.

Previous: Linear light slots frame the shelving units creating a strong formality to the rhythm of the space. Linear LEDs set behind glass diffusers provide good volumes of general light balancing the daylight entering from the west. Directional downlights highlight artworks creating well balanced focal points.

Opposite: Within the lower ground home cinema discreet lighting is required so as not to distract from or reflect off the television. A glass shelf sits behind the sofa with linear LEDs recessed 100mm below to allow for diffusion. The shelf is practical allowing for placement of drinks and provides the decorative function of subtly accentuating the wallpaper.

Light as we perceive it is most clearly manifested in a rainbow. A single white prism split into multiple colours is the visible section of the electromagnetic spectrum with ultraviolet and infrared light at either end. A rainbow consists of red, orange, yellow, green, blue, indigo and violet electromagnetic waves. The impact of most sections of the electromagnetic spectrum is well-documented, such as radiation from infrared light or the burning penetration of ultraviolet. Less understood is how we respond to individual wavelengths of light within the visible spectrum. This exciting and expanding area of research holds the key to further scientific discoveries.

It's a good thing that when God created the rainbow he didn't consult a decorator or he would still be picking colours.

Sam Levenson

Above and opposite: Subtle changes in colour transform a lower ground pool. With the ability to mimic daylight, artificial light becomes king of the shadows, dancing over the darkness, revealing form and texture.

Understanding our psychological and physiological responses to light will form the foundation for illuminating the enlightened home. Discovering how you feel about light, how you respond to varying light conditions from the brilliance of the midday sun to the soft dappled rays of sunset will assist you in developing your lighting scheme.

Questions you might ask yourself: What is your favourite seat in the house? Is it next to a burning fire or placed within the conservatory? Do you dim the lights when entering a room or switch them to full brightness? When do you feel happiest, most relaxed, excited? Analyse the lighting, both natural and artificial for each of these moments. If you are inspired by bright mornings, would it be beneficial to have an east-facing bedroom so that you can appreciate sunrise to its fullest? Perhaps you are more inspired by the neon extravaganza of a city at night? A darker space, with high contrast and colour may be preferable.

Opposite and above right: Discreet floor uplights graze the underside of this sculptural staircase revealing the textured stone work. Low level lights from the ground to the lower ground floor highlight the treads creating a pathway of light. The step lights complement the wonderful volume of natural light and reduce the need for lighting on the half landings.

Although we may naturally be more lark or owl, the rhythm of life was until modern times driven by the presence and absence of light. Every living being has an internal biological clock, described as our circadian rhythm. These internal clocks, in tune with the pattern of the day, are hugely affected by the presence or absence of daylight. With our 24-hour lifestyles, including shift work, long office hours and jet lag, a lack of access to daylight can have a detrimental effect on our health. Artificial light, so readily available, has had the greatest impact on our lifestyles over the last 100 years.

The eyes have a critical role to play in our path to well-being. The discovery of a third receptor confirmed that light exerts a biochemical effect on our internal pathways. Light's non-visual effect on the body is via the pineal gland where it is converted into neurotransmitters directly impacting our hormonal responses and circadian system. We know that it is easier to get up in the summer with bright light streaming through windows and that in winter, with the onset of darkness, we start to feel tired earlier in the day. There is scientific evidence showing that certain wave lengths of visible light have a greater impact on our circadian rhythms. It is with this knowledge and the understanding of the critical role daylight plays within our lives that we should be designing our homes.

Above: Daylight is of a premium in this room at ground level. The use of artificial supplementary light provided by the horizontal shadow gap above the bed affords a balanced level of light within the space during daylight hours. The evergreen vertical wall of the small courtyard provides a feeling of being connected to nature, overriding any awareness of not being able to see the sky.

Opposite: The kitchen and dining room are placed on the first floor of this mews house to optimise available daylight. Reflective polished surfaces and internal windows allow the light to bounce further into the room, preventing the depth of the house from feeling flat and lifeless.

We have a strong need for visual stimulation so that we remain engaged with our surroundings. We desensitise to our environment very quickly and become bored and disengaged if there is no movement or change. Critically, artificial lighting can become a tool to create, through variances in colour or quantity, conditions which are able to stimulate responses from us. Dynamic lighting, a popular new term, is in essence the ability to vary lighting conditions, whether through simple dimmers, colour tunability or varying circuits.

Natural dynamic movements of light include the softening of shadows at sunset, the dance of wind and light as they reflect and ripple over water and the flicker of candlelight across someone's face. These subtle moments in time captivate us due to their dynamic essence. Can you imagine a fire without flicker? A day without sunlight and shadows? A night sky without stars? Contrast and variance, night and day, light and shadow—these are the creative ingredients to a healthier and more interesting world.

Increasingly we will see the introduction of biodynamic lighting within the home. These intelligent systems mimic daylight creating shifts in output and colour temperature according to the time of day. Biodynamic lighting has gathered favour from hospitals where patient recovery times have been reduced, in schools where improved concentration levels and reading speeds have been noted, and in prisons with a reduction in aggressive behaviour. Disruption to our circadian rhythms and lack of daylight contributes to a host of physical conditions such as

Seasonal Affective Disorder (SAD), obesity, cancer, diabetes and depression. In the future, biodynamic light therapy and access to daylight will be considered essential to the recuperation of all patients.

By understanding the critical role daylight performs in our perception of the world, the spaces we inhabit and the people we meet, we can begin to study how to manipulate and embrace this wonderful medium in order to optimise our physical and emotional well-being.

Our culture, traditions and customs influence our relationship with light providing us with a unique set of sensory experiences. With this understanding of our responses to light we can embrace a design philosophy that enables us to unlock its exceptional power.

Above: The soft lines of the coffer ceiling work in harmony with the linear diffusion beneath the floating shelf of the fireplace. The warmth of the fire's burning embers creates a more intimate space at night.

Opposite: The geometric pendants provide sparkle and fun to the breakfast room. The open lattice steel allows for efficient light distribution and striking patterns of light to reach the ceiling.

The Philosophy of Lighting Design

The philosophy of lighting design should incorporate a holistic and systematic approach, incorporating the fundamental architectural, historical and cultural elements whilst ensuring the inhabitants remain at its pivotal point. This human-centric focus prioritises a family's needs.

The lighting designer's first task is to visualise the complex spaces which we inhabit, including the subtle details and variances of materials, textures and colours. The designer is then able to assess the client's requirements to further define a hierarchy amongst this diverse physical and emotional palette.

By creating focal points and introducing layers of light, the designer is able to capture the essence of both the architectural and interior elements. This structured approach of reading the architecture through layers whilst satisfying emotional needs creates a formality and relationships within the home. In a similar manner, an artist paints the theatre of life, accentuating the mid, fore and background with highlights and shadows creating the illusion of depth and drama. It is this invisible organisation, highly considered and creatively balanced, that allows a piece of art or room to feel so inviting.

Below and opposite: The architecture is accentuated with linear details which run from the changing rooms through to the pool. Lighting is integrated within the joinery creating a modern feel to a more traditional design. A Swarovski crystal fibre-optic ceiling provides a pretty and playful addition.

Intelligent design should prioritise the human experience and optimise our sense of well-being. This human-centric philosophy ensures our focus on lighting begins with an understanding of daylight and the orientation of the space to be lit: north, south, east or west. By discovering when and where sunlight penetrates a room you can organise its associated functions. If daylight needs to be maximised, then the introduction of skylights, light pipes or lighter coloured, reflective furniture will need to be considered. By contrast, a house blessed with an abundance of daylight will require daylight control and shielding from the sun's rays with brise soleils, exterior planting, pagodas, window treatments, and careful placement of artwork and furniture.

Understanding how natural light informs a space allows us to concentrate on its complement, artificial light. Many rooms where tasks are undertaken require daylight to be permanently supplemented by artificial light. To design with artificial light, it is helpful to breakdown the different types of lighting required. Residential lighting design is often broken down into four categories: (1) General or ambient lighting which is diffuse, indirect light that fills the volume of a room; (2) Accent lighting which defines a space or object; (3) Task lighting which allows us to fulfil an activity efficiently and safely; and lastly (4) Decorative lighting, described as 'architectural jewellery' and creatively used to personalise a space.

These categories are very useful when considering the priorities of a space. A sitting room may require decorative and accent lighting whilst a kitchen or bathroom may require task and general lighting. Occasionally, you may wish to also consider emergency lighting, which is particularly useful in areas where there are regular power cuts or in large houses with more complex escape routes. Discreet integrated emergency battery packs can provide emergency light for up to an hour creating safe routes through stairwells. Security lighting, often linked to Passive Infrared Detectors (PIRs) and photocells for operation only when activated from dusk are usually provided by specialists. Safety lighting should be considered around steps used at night, pools and water features.

The skill of a lighting designer is in being able to visualise a space, to read a room as a series of elevated planes. The walls and vertical surfaces become the canvas to be highlighted or lost to the shadow. Our focus as lighting designers is steered in the same direction as the priority of our visual field. 80 per cent of what we view in a space is at eye level. Therefore the easiest and most comfortable focal points will be those that lie within this angle of view. Focal points, particularly artwork, are often at eye level, centred on our visual field. Think how quickly we view a room. Our eyes rarely look to the floor or ceiling, unless they are drawn there by low-level lighting or a dazzling chandelier. Most of what we see will be in our direct line of sight. It is therefore important to consider how will we 'dress' this line of sight. How will the light graze and fall on these objects? Do we desire uniformity or pockets of definition that will draw us to look closer at what is being lit?

Free yourself from constraints; the home is now your stage. Allow the theatre of your inhabitants' lives to become the players, as they move around and require different lighting depending on the mood or task required. Think differently. Decorative lighting, whether in the form of pendants, sconces or neon installations becomes more than a source of light—it is an emotional medium which will engage our senses. Be brave. Treasured artwork, sculpture and family heirlooms become emotional highlights within a well illuminated space. The key to balancing the light within a home is to ensure the layers of light work with the hierarchy of functions required, such as using task, accent, general and decorative lighting, or architecturally, layering the light onto the most important surfaces or emotionally connecting to different treasures.

Picture Lighting

Below left: The artwork is gently illuminated through the diffuse light of the lamp.

Below right: A singular discreet directional downlight highlights the artwork, ensuring the piece becomes the focal point when seated.

Opposite: Two directional downlights crosslight the large photograph ensuring it is well-lit. The reflected light assists with the task lighting to light the kitchen work surface. A small adjustable surface spotlight, mounted to the concrete beam accentuates the smaller canvas ensuring it holds our attention.

What is the correct way to light art? Experience confirms that the answer is both emotive and subjective. Do you recreate the vast even illumination of an artist's studio, pin spot perfectly with a framing projector, create discreet scollops of light accentuating individual pieces or embrace the wonderful tradition of the picture light. All these methods work well and can be applied with varying success depending on a number of factors. These include whether the artwork is framed, glazed, acrylic, pencil or oil, traditional or modern, as well as most importantly the context in and on which the painting sits.

The humble picture light can elevate a simple picture to the realm of a grand master. Picture lights assist in creating layers of ambient light supplementing the diffused illumination of table lamps and chandeliers. The advancements in LED technology with tinier light sources, superb colour rendering and advancement in optics have ensured picture lights compete with other techniques to light art.

The directional downlight will remain popular, as basic trigonometry allows you to calculate the position of the light fitting in relation to its angle of tilt, size of artwork and the height of the ceiling. This simple mathematics or formula is often ignored, even though it is the only method which allows you to work out the correct distance off the wall to light your art beautifully.

Downlights are often set in a grid-like formation with little consideration for what they might be lighting. Their position is critical to the success of your lighting scheme. A well-positioned spotlight will accent a piece of art or sculpture, light a bowl of fruit, highlight a beautifully laid table and create focal points in a home. The smallest, most carefully positioned downlight can pack a big punch when placed correctly. The pricey powerhouse of the art world will always be the framing projector, a fitting installed and commissioned by specialists to highlight the exact dimensions of the painting or sculpture so there is no light spill.

Track lighting provides the most flexible solution for lighting art. Multiple spotlights and wall washers are easily combined utilising multiple circuits to ensure optimal results.

There are many ways to light art, from diffuse daylight to the soft glow of a table lamp. However, the most dramatic impression will be where the lighting appears to have played the smallest part.

Circuits

A lighting circuit is a switched path round which current flows—you cannot have one light source on two circuits, though you do get fittings with individual light sources that can be switched separately. Flexibility is key when circuiting your home. We are drawn to light, like moths to the flame, so ensure the brightest point, the focal point, is on its own circuit. You may wish to circuit your lighting as you have 'layered' it, whether through function, hierarchy or the position. Each layer will require a separate switch. The human brain often struggles with more than four switches on any one switch plate. If you require more, consider a pre-set control system or invest in home automation. These more advanced solutions, which can create a pathway of light throughout the home from the touch of one button, provide master off switches, replay your lighting when you are on holiday and provide savings in energy usage. Daylight sensors, PIRs and blind controls can also be easily integrated providing greater ease of use.

Above and opposite: This minimal apartment with its long internal hallway utilises two circuits to control the lighting. The first circuit provides a low level pathway of light linking the family space to the bedrooms. A discreet downlight highlighting the singular piece of art is also linked to this circuit. The second circuit, or switch-line, includes the vertical shadow gap which creates a visual pause to the long wall. Linked to this circuit is the same linear LED light fitting but used horizontally above the cupboards. The 10W/m 2700k linear LED tape emits a soft, diffuse reflected light into the space.

Architecture is the learned game,
correct and magnificent,
of forms assembled in the light.

Le Corbusier

Lighting Design

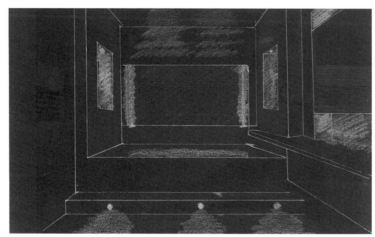

In designing a lighting scheme it is useful to create a list of questions: What is the space primarily used for and who will be the users? What tasks will be undertaken? Are there architectural constraints, concrete ceilings, steel joists, pipework or air conditioning ducts? Is it a listed building? What is the furniture layout and the colours, textures and fabrics to be used? Are there any important pieces of artwork or large items of furniture such as bookcases or armoires? Once answered, these questions will provide useful data and allow you to add significant pieces of furniture, art and structural elements to your lighting plans to ensure they are remembered and addressed when designing your lighting scheme.

Light, both artificial and natural, will transform a space. Room dimensions appear to change with small rooms becoming open and airy with large volumes of diffuse light, whilst large open plan spaces become cosier and more inviting with intimate layers of light centred around seating. In narrow corridors, illuminate one wall with an asymmetric wash of light to push

the wall outwards expanding the space. Where the architecture is dull introduce playful non-symmetric lighting details and if the budget is tight, explore the high street stores and websites for less expensive fittings.

The phenomena of light is difficult to describe, and lighting designers use many tools, from sketches and models, to lighting and photo editing software, to try and communicate the effects they are trying to achieve. These more advanced options are often time-consuming to create. Quick sketches and inspirational images pulled from websites and magazines alongside a clear description will capture the spirit of light just as well. Discover your own language of light, a descriptive array of adjectives will convey the atmosphere you are trying to create, from bright, radiant, sparkling and energetic to diffuse, diaphanous and translucent. These will serve you well as you describe your vision and the ambiance required.

Above top left and right: SketchUp, a quick and easy to learn software tool has been used to create a daylight simulation of the bedroom. If required this could be further enhanced with photo editing software for accuracy and detailing.

Above bottom left and right: The daylight model has been enhanced with a lighting plug-in to simulate the effect of the linear LED, downlights and bedside lamps. Beware! The more realistic the visuals, the greater the expectation will be from the client. Simple sketches often work best to convey ideas and effects.

Opposite top left and right: A quick hand sketch can convey very quickly the effects you wish to achieve. Often these simple perspectives will provide greater clarity to the design team.

Opposite bottom left and right: An alternative is to keep black paper and a white pencil with you. These informal sketches highlight the layers of light and the variety of effects to be achieved.

Overleaf: Fibre-optic tails gather in glass balls. This is a close up shot of a large colour changing chandelier.

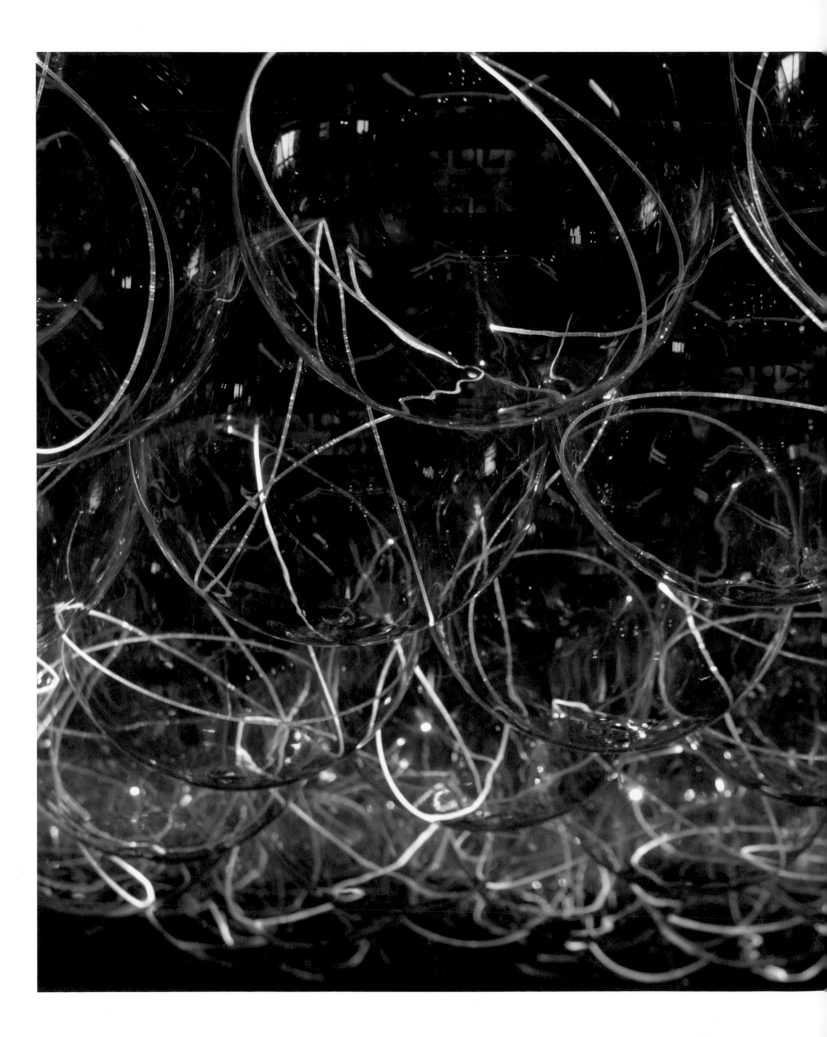

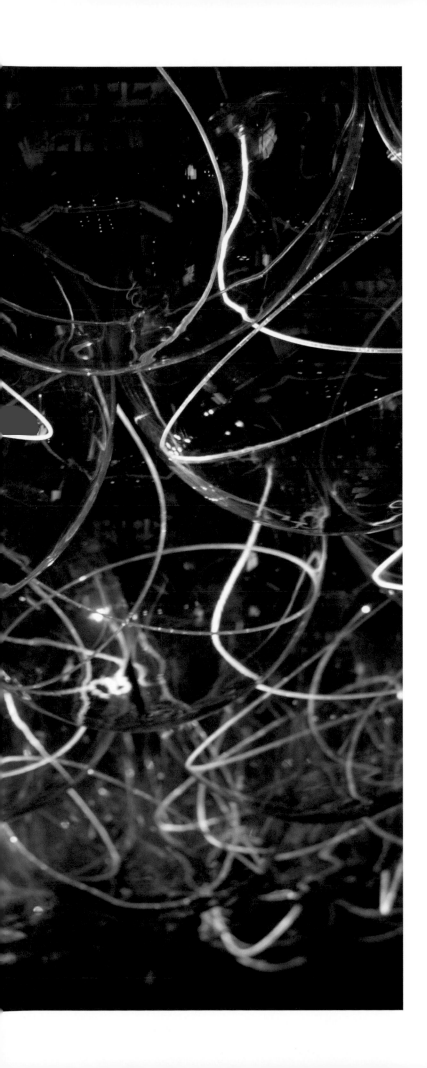

Lighting Design Technology

A New Language of Light

Lighting technology is advancing at an unprecedented rate, creating new terminology and a wealth of design possibilities. From watts (W) to lumens (lm), colour rendering to the colour quality scale, there is a new dialogue. The global concern with energy consumption and increasing bills has ensured an active interest from the consumer. The market is filled with energy efficient products, so the focus has now turned to the quality of light available, colour rendering and tuneability, adjustable beam widths and compatibility.

Colour Rendering Index

The Colour Rendering Index (CRI) is a quantitative measure of how accurately the colour of surfaces appear, compared to daylight under various artificial light sources. Colour Rendering is measured on the Rendering Index out of 100 (in Ra). The sun has a CRI of 100. For artificial light an Ra of between 80–85 is reasonable (most LEDs), 85–89 is good, whilst a figure between 90–100 is excellent. Halogen with a high CRI of 98 has become the holy grail for LED technology. The main issue with the CRI is that it measures a light source against only eight colours whereby the newer Colour Quality Scale (CQS) measures over 15 colours providing a more accurate indication of how we perceive lit objects.

Colour Quality Scale

The Colour Quality Scale (CQS) is a method of accurately measuring how the colour of surfaces appear using a standard number of 15 colour samples. The standard 15 test colour samples which include saturated and skin tone colours are shown below.

Ra	R1	R2	R3	R4	R5	R6	R7	R8	R9	R10	R11	R12	R13	R14	R15

Colour Temperature

The colour temperature of light is an indication of the appearance of light and is measured in degrees Kelvin (k). A lower temperature in degrees Kelvin ensures a 'warmer' appearance, a higher temperature indicates a 'cooler' appearance. A popular colour temperature in traditional homes is 2,700k, however, more contemporary spaces might prefer 3,000k and gyms 3,500–4,000k. The flexibility to vary colour temperatures through one light source, comparable to halogen when dimmed, has many benefits. The cooler colour temperatures, like the noon sun, can improve concentration, efficacy and create a more productive working environment. Warmer colour temperatures, akin to sunset, provide a softer, more atmospheric ambience.

8000K

7500K

7000K

66500K

6000K

5500K

5000K

4500K

4000K

3500K

3000K

2500K

2000K

1500K

1000K

Above left: Linear 2,700k LEDs set beneath the sauna benches and within the shadow gap accentuate the warmth of the wood.

Above right: Small LEDs are set at low level with linear LEDs set beneath the floating seat. Swarovski crystals are fed with fibre-optics to create a magical hypnotic effect.

Opposite left and right: The far left photo illustrates colour hyper-optimisation where certain hues can gain greater depth through choice of specialist lamps, creating a greater intensity within certain wavelengths. The right-hand photo illustrates the effect of using lamps with poor colour rendering, colours are washed out and clarity of textures is reduced.

Lamp Efficacy

Great importance has been placed on the efficacy of a light source and its life expectancy. A simple calculation for the efficacy of a lamp is measured by dividing the total lamp light output in lumens by the power consumed in watts. For example, a 2W LED which emits 100lm would have an efficacy of 50 lumens per circuit-watt—a circuit-watt being the total power consumed in a lighting circuit by the lamp and its control gear. Lumen is used to describe the quantity of light emitted by a source. A 100W incandescent lamp emits approximately 1,200–1,600lm, a 60W incandescent 800lm. Luminous efficacy is a measure of how effective a lamp is in transforming electricity into light measured in lumens per watt (lm/W).

The focus on efficient light sources has often overlooked the efficacy of the lighting scheme as a whole. Grids of downlights provide a uniform distribution of light but often fail to provide light where it is needed most such as task areas. Controls and multiple circuits are often an afterthought. Generous circuiting ensures flexibility of use as well as the option of only using the lights required. By combining the optimisation of daylight, utilising energy efficient lamps and providing dimmers, PIR and other control measures, we are able to design ever more efficient lighting schemes.

Below and opposite: LEDs are used extensively throughout the home. Clients with their focus on reducing energy consumption no longer view them as a compromise but as the way forward.

Light Sources

An overview of the common light sources found within the home provides the advantages and disadvantages of each.

Incandescent lamps, which are slowly being phased out, are popular due to being inexpensive, dimmable and having excellent colour rendering. The main disadvantage is their inefficiency (12lm/W) and poor lamp life (1,000 hours).

The halogen lamp, a bright, compact source with excellent colour rendering averages a 3,000 hour lamp life. The disadvantage of this popular light source is that it becomes very hot in operation and is inefficient in converting electricity into light with an average efficacy of 25lm/W.

Fluorescent lamps are efficient and offer great lamp life, averaging 15,000 hours, though often suffer from poorer colour rendering and disposal issues relating to their mercury content.

The light-emitting diode (LED) is highly efficient, has excellent life expectancy, averaging 50,000 hours plus and low heat. The disadvantages include the higher initial price, dimming compatibility and often poor colour rendering. All LEDs require control gear called a driver, which feeds the LEDs with the correct voltage. Drivers are normally 12V or 24V or constant current ranging from 350mA, 700mA, to 1,000mA. All drivers have a maximum and minimum load, as well as a maximum distance from the LED to the driver, which will vary depending on the power and number of LEDs connected to it. If an LED is dimmable a dimming controller is often required in combination

with the driver though some manufacturers combine the two. Dimming can be via mains or via 1–10V, DALI (Digital Addressable Lighting Interface) or DMX (Digital Multiplex).

The easy introduction of colour is one of the many advantages of LEDs. This is often abbreviated to RGB, which stands for the red, green and blue diodes. A more advanced spectrum is utilised with RGBAW—this is the introduction of white and amber LEDs which assist in a more subtle and wider colour palette. If utilising colour change, an RGB controller is required in combination with the driver. RGB dimming can be via 1-10V with three circuits required, DMX or DALI.

Drivers can be wired in series which divides the total power supply between the LEDs or in parallel which means that each LED will receive the total voltage from the power supply.

LEDs are available as point source, with reflectors providing beams of light or linear often referred to as LED strip lights or tape. These long, flexible strips of LEDs can be cut to precise lengths and are often used in cabinetry and coves or architectural details. Linear LEDs often benefit from being placed in diffusers. This protects them, acts as a heat sink and creates an easy way to install them with the use of clips or adhesive tape.

OLEDs (Organic Light-Emitting Diodes) are still in their infancy and are available in various colours as panels that emit light. These are still predominantly used in decorative or sculptural applications due to their low output and efficacy.

Controlling Your Environment

Intelligent controls will dominate the future of our homes and consistently monitor our environment to ensure optimum use and potential savings in electricity consumption. From simple PIRs with integrated photocells and time clocks to predictive systems which 'learn' our patterns of behaviour, the house of the future will be more responsive and intuitive towards our needs.

Dimming lights ensure balanced light levels, reduced energy consumption and greater flexibility. There is a significant number of dimming techniques available, each one best suited to a particular light source. Compatibility between the light source and dimmer is key.

Standard rotary dimmers, whose disadvantages include only allowing you to dim from one location, as well as having a minimum and maximum load per circuit. The issues arise when this is ignored as it is possible to both under and over run a dimmer.

Momentary button dimming allows you to dim from more than one location—this works very well in bedrooms, hallways and stairwells, however, clients often find them less intuitive than rotary dimmers.

There are various ways to dim LEDs, traditionally 1–10V dimming has been popular but this requires an additional cable to be run from the dimmer module to the driver. If a house is pre-wired or first fix undertaken this is more likely to be a problem. New mains dimmable LED drivers have hit the market and are proving popular precisely for those unable to run an additional dimming cable.

DMX allows us to control, dim and programme colour. DMX addresses vary from simple plug and play to large complex installations.

PIRs which detect a person moving into a space are popular in utility and downstairs powder rooms. Linked to time clocks, they allow immediate operation for a set time without the need of a switch. More advanced features allow integration with photocells and astronomical time clocks to ensure lights are only operated if daylight is not sufficient or at specific times if activated.

Photocells, or daylight sensors, should be applied to all exterior lighting circuits ensuring outdoor lighting only operates from dusk and for a fixed period showing consideration to neighbours and local wildlife.

Product Specification

Opposite: The large pendant draws the eye away from the narrow, high ceiling room by creating a striking focal point. The mid-layer is accentuated with the vertical blue light slot. Natural light fills the background preventing the room from feeling too small.

Selecting the correct lighting product can feel like searching for a needle in a haystack. However, a little organisation goes a long way. Firstly, consider how much light you need. Start by thinking in lumens (volume of light required from a light source) as this will immediately provide a framework for your search. Secondly, consider the beam angle of light, which measures in degrees of how wide the light is spread: are you looking for wide, uniform distribution or a pin spot of light to focus onto flowers? Most manufacturers offer a limited range including narrow (8–12°), medium (18–32°), wide (38–40°), flood (60°), and elliptical (12°x80°). Thirdly, identify your chosen colour temperature. Few manufacturers offer much below 2,700k and be warned that many manufacturers will still call 3,000k fixtures 'warm white' as they do not offer 2,700k as an option. The required CRI will further define your search as the light fixtures available with a CRI above 90 are still in relatively short supply. The fourth option will be the IP rating or ingress protection required—is the fixture located near water or in a humid environment? Lastly, control: how are you going to dim your fittings, what drivers are available, how many will you need and where will they be placed? Are they small enough to fit through the cut-out of the fixture or will they need to sit remotely? Once your product is selected the specification sheet will be required for your electrician.

A manufacturer's product specification sheet should contain the following information: (1) An image of the product and ideally photos of it being used in situ; (2) Dimensions of the product including recess depth required and cut-outs; (3) Lumen packages, beam widths, colour temperature, available CRIs and driver requirements; (4) Product finishes and order codes including accessories. Occasionally you will also receive dimming compatibility charts along with the LED chip manufacturer, which is also useful.

LEDs will continue to transform the world of lighting with continued improvements in CRI and efficacy. However, they are also becoming communication devices that monitor our every move, transmitting data and opening up a new world which is yet to be fully conceived. 'The Internet of Everything' buzzes and light fittings are being targeted to assist with this easy transmission of data. Further research studies should also help to ensure not only a brighter and more efficient future but a healthier one as well. With an increased understanding of the power of the sun maybe now we can start to study in more depth the health benefits which could be provided by its artificial counterpart.

Colour, Materials and Texture

Colour, Materials and Texture

Our experience of light, colour, materials and texture is heavily influenced by the culture, traditions, art, design and literature of our times. Historically, the palette of colours and light sources used have been dictated by the materials available. Contemporary technology has created a wealth of possibilities so why do we so often choose to live with white plastered walls? Our experience of light, intimately related to our emotional and sensory perception of space, is informed by the choice of colour, materiality and textures used. In our kaleidoscopic world with almost infinite technological possibilities, will our choices change?

The psychology of colour is a fascinating and complex subject, yet it is still little understood and occasionally deemed unscientific. Many questions remain unanswered. Does colour exist without light? What is colour if it is not perceived? Why does a white room appear bright? Are apples more appealing when sat next to oranges? Why do girls prefer pink and boys blue?

Below and opposite: The simple palette of materials is enhanced with the use of colour. A linear red LED accentuates the change in floor levels and links through to the accent colours used elsewhere. A soft blue LED set above the bedroom wall provides the feeling of twilight within the adjacent bathroom space.

As lighting designers we are able to establish ground rules to aid our understanding of light, colour and the perception of space. For example, we know that darker colours absorb more light whilst lighter, glossier surfaces will reflect the most. We understand the importance of the spectral composition of light. When we light a material, for example denim, the denim will reflect back to us only the blue spectrum of light as all the other wavelengths of light are absorbed by the material. To increase the perceived blueness and vibrancy of the denim, we could add more blue to our white light or use a pure blue light. The colour temperature and colour rendering of a light source will both have a huge impact on the appearance of an object. Poor colour rendering will often create a distorted and washed out world that is very disorientating and disturbing to the human psyche. Warm colour temperatures (1,800k–3,000k) will aid finishes in the warmer colour spectrum—the reds, oranges and yellows. Cooler colour temperatures (3,000k–6,500k) will optimise the blues and greens. With this basic understanding we are able to make more informed choices. However, colour is often considered as an afterthought and as decoration, as opposed to an intrinsic element of the architecture. This is surprising given the power of colour, its effect on our environment and sense of well-being.

Our responses to colour and light are heavily subjective—a blue room may feel calm and peaceful to some yet suffocating and claustrophobic to others. The perception of colour is also greatly influenced by the varying quality of natural light available as well as the context and framework in which the colours sit.

Left, below and opposite: RGB LED asymmetric wall washers create a rainbow of colours within the pool room. The solidity of colour creates form, defining the space with dramatic vibrancy further enhanced by the still water's power of reflection.

Materials:
Absorption and Reflection

Mirrors, high gloss and metallic or lacquered surfaces reflect light, and these reflective surfaces are often used by designers to help lift light levels within a space. Reflective surfaces are defined as those that reflect most of the light that falls upon them. This could be a white lacquered wardrobe or polished marble countertop, a mirrored window reveal or the use of an external reflection pool. Careful positioning of the light source is required if using highly reflective surfaces as one will see the source, and this can cause unwanted glare.

Areas of concern are plinth lights reflecting off highly polished floors, shelf lighting in lacquered or mirror-backed bookcases and under cabinet lighting being seen in the polished work top. Dark, matt or textured surfaces absorb most of the light with a matt black surface absorbing all light that falls upon it. Dark materials, even when well-lit will appear dark, as no amount of artificial light will make a room with dark walls appear bright. This simple fact is often overlooked or ignored when choosing a colour and material pallet for a room.

Sensory Impact of Textures

Texture is described as the surface quality of a material, from the roughness of an exposed brick wall, the sheen of a silk velvet sofa to the ribbed undulation of a bathroom tile. We are drawn to discovering the tactile experience of texture, as a well-lit surface provides both visual and sensory stimulation. Textured surfaces can be further enhanced through the grazing of light. This well established and dramatic lighting technique provides an additional dimension to a space. We are drawn to the sensory experience of touching materials grazed with light, to investigate further the rawness of exposed concrete or the undulating grain of sawn wood. This discovery further enhances our emotional perception of the space in which we live.

Colour, light and texture provide the emotional content of a space, deeply entwined and dancing to the same tune, they enhance our experience and improve our sense of well-being.

Below: A warm white, linear LED, (2,700k, 10W/m) is used within the coffered ceiling. The gentle illumination defines the symmetry of the space. A neutral colour palette is enhanced with luxurious materials in a range of textures.

Opposite left: The mirrored table reflects the chandelier and coffered ceiling.

Opposite right: The textured mirrors either side of the fireplace create interesting reflections and refractions of light adding sparkle and brilliance to the space.

Beauty lies not in objects,
but in the interaction between the shadow
and the light created by objects.

Junichiro Tanizaki, *In Praise of Shadows*

Above and left: A crystal chandelier cascades through the stairwell mirroring its form. Lit from above, the brilliant crystals shimmer and glisten ensuring the dramatic piece takes centre stage.

Opposite: An antique mirror frames the powder room. Vertical shadow gaps lighten the space whilst decorative wall lights create warmth and glamour.

I sense Light as the giver of all presences, and material as spent Light. What is made by Light casts a shadow, and the shadow belongs to Light.

Louis Kahn

Lighting Techniques

Designers draw upon a palette of lighting design techniques, often obliquely referenced as 'light effects'. Clarity of definitions within the profession is scarce with many terms used interchangeably. Classification for our purpose will be aesthetic as opposed to empirical. Light, although measurable, is most easily understood when perceived within the fabric of a building whether through architectural slots, shadow gaps and coffers, or more decorative elements. It is therefore in this manner that this chapter unfolds.

LEDs have become the primary light source within our homes. Their small size has enabled many lighting techniques to be reimagined and embraced. Before considering a lighting technique ask: What are you trying to emphasise? Are you looking to accentuate and reveal, or divert and conceal? Is a strong rhythm or pattern required to supplement the architecture? Is assistance required with supplementing natural light levels or a visual task?

Light, God's eldest daughter, is a principal beauty in a building.

Thomas Fuller

Previous: A shadow gap delineates the junction between plaster and brickwork creating a sense of lightness to the framework of the room. Linear light slots, centred on the mirrors provide superb volumes of general light.

Opposite: The home cinema with multiple coffers, shadow gaps and linear light details has been laid out with the latest in home technology. A powerful control system is installed to enhance the audiovisual experience, an effect immersing the peripheral vision so that the colour and sound become one with the room. A patented sound to light and video to light technology creates an environment of subtly changing light in synchronicity to the imagery of the film. This immersive technology can be turned on and off at ease reverting to layers of soft white light when required (as shown).

Coffer Ceiling

In architecture, a coffer is a sunken panel, usually a square or rectangle to mirror the shape of a room. This detail is created by either a cut-out within a ceiling or by dropping the perimeter of the ceiling allowing for the light source to be concealed.

Coffers, occasionally called cove lighting, provide an architectural frame to a space and an increased sense of ceiling height. A visual emphasis is created through illumination of the architecture by concealing the light source which is discreetly positioned inside the dropped perimeter. The effect is a diffused wash of light travelling up into the 'raised' section of the ceiling. The greater the available depth to uplight increases the softness of the effect.

Below: The coffer ceiling reflects the shape of the kitchen island creating interest by breaking up the ceiling of the large open plan space.

Opposite: The formality of the drawing room is emphasised by the symmetry of the coffer ceiling. The diffused light emitted by the linear LED in the coffer creates a volume of light in the centre of the room. Table lamps frame the seating spaces providing additional task light.

The fireplace becomes the focal point using directed light to enhance the asymmetric framing of the shelves and art. An LED has been placed within the curtain slot to light the silk fabric and frame the view to the garden during the day.

Coffer Ceiling Detail

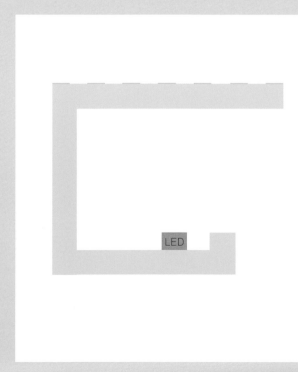

LED

Early planning is essential when introducing coffered ceilings. The scale should be carefully thought through and details such as purchasing pre-made profiles discussed and priced at the outset of project.

If higher light levels are required then use lighter coloured paint within the raised ceiling to create an effective reflective surface. However, darker and metallic finishes also look superb. If integrating air conditioning or other methods of ventilation within the dropped section be aware of the finish of the grilles. The upstand is built to conceal the light source as well as potentially unsightly air conditioning vents, cables and control gear. The height of the upstand will also dictate the cut-off of light emitted, ideally it will sit in line with the top of the light source. An upstand or pre-made aluminium profile ensures a clean finish though careful attention should still be made to the inside of the coffer which is often left as bare plasterboard. If the inside of a coffer is not painted then inconsistencies in light output will occur.

Linear LEDs are most often used to create this effect, and further choices will include use of profiles, colour tunability, colour change and light output. Practical considerations will also include where to conceal drivers so that they are accessible but not visible.

Shadow Gaps

A shadow gap is an architectural detail where an intended 'gap' is left in the joint between two surfaces. An example of this would be where a ceiling and a wall meet, or two walls when set vertically to create a shadow instead of a joint.

Ceilings are often dropped to create this effect with the gap running around the perimeter or along one side of the room. Shadow gaps are often used to integrate wall grazing effects as well as more diffused and softer perimeters of light.

Vertical shadow gaps are an excellent technique for elegantly lighting up the corners of rooms and delineating long spaces with punctuations of light. The effect is to accentuate the architectural form of the room and increase general light levels.

To create a shadow gap, a light source is positioned inside the dropped perimeter behind a small upstand. In hiding the light source you see a diffused wash of light reflected off the wall.

Below: The linear LED, set above the kitchen units and within the clerestory window complement the linearity of the shadow gap opposite and assist with additional layers of light.

Opposite: The shadow gap accentuates the architecture and brings diffuse general light to the centre of this deep space. Downlights set centred over the kitchen islands ensure excellent task light.

Shadow Gap Detail

The 150mm (5.9in) rule is used as a general starting point in which to form many of the linear details shown. Previously, with the dominant use of fluorescent lamps, 150mm allowed for easy accessibility, maintenance and optimum diffusion of light. With the longer lamp life of LEDs, varying light outputs and smaller profiles this rule does not need to be strictly adhered to.

For flexibility and to create a more dynamic environment consider using LEDs with different colour temperatures or a colour tuneable light source so the effect can be varied at different times. This technique is often used in hotel lobbies to create a crisp bright ambience during the day and a softer warmer effect at night.

Downlights, as well as linear lighting, can be integrated within a shadow gap. This works well when highlighting textured walls and helps to keep the ceilings clutter free.

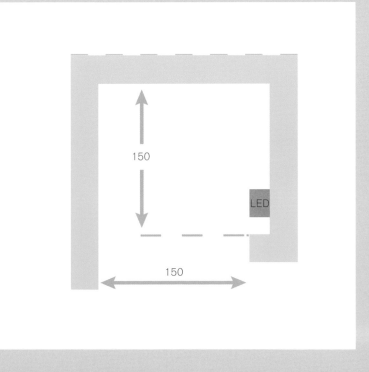

Above and opposite: A shadow gap has been used within the stairwell of a contemporary home by cantilevering the stairs from the wall. The soft light set onto the vertical rear face of the staircase landing emits light in both directions. The diffuse effect is warm and welcoming, adding interest and softness to the strong architectural language.

Opposite top: Low level lights complement the discreet effect by continuing a soft pathway of light to the bedrooms.

Light Slots

Light slots are linear cuts mounted into or upon the framework of the architecture. These provide interest through the creation of rhythm and drama. In basements, the soft diffuse reflected light can create the illusion of natural light falling through a skylight or window.

In spaces with restricted ceiling voids, light slots are often set vertically within walls and can be custom built on site. The slot may also house fans, air conditioning and speakers which reduces the effect of ceiling clutter. It is a contemporary, practical and energy efficient method of providing clean, architectural volumes of light into a space. If further directional light is required then spotlights should be introduced within the slot.

Light Slots Detail

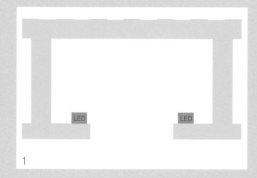

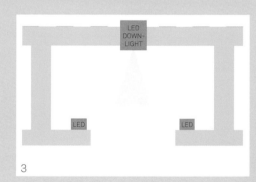

1. A simple light slot with LEDs mounted on both sides allowing for two separate circuits with LEDs of different colour temperatures creating different effects and volumes of light throughout the day.

2. A minimal light slot with clean architectural detailing. To ensure the effect is as minimal as possible, place the LEDs on the side which will be least seen.

3. Light slots can house multiple effects and ensure the ceiling plane remains free from clutter. If ceiling depth allows then additional downlights can be recessed within the slot to create crisp accent light or assist in increasing general light levels when required. Many manufacturers provide pre-made profiles where the downlights are able to slide on an internal track for maximum flexibility.

Above and opposite: The images illustrate a contemporary entrance to a warehouse. Curved panels conceal an irregular sloping wall and steel joists. A warm white LED sits alongside an RGB LED strip. This ensures maximum flexibility when choosing to create a wash of soft colours within the space. A linear LED set within the blind slot provides a soft delineation to the window treatment.

Above and left: A linear light slot doubles up as the handrail as it ascends the curved staircase over three flights. The linear effect mirrors the shadow detail accentuating the beautiful stone treads. On the lower ground floor a soft linear light is thrown on to the wine racks below.

Opposite: The pendant grounds the breakfast table with an ambient glow. This subtle overhead light is primarily decorative, creating a punctuation mark before the view.

Light slots are created within the steel framework. A 2,700k linear LED is concealed to create this diffuse effect. Additional task lighting has been recessed within the ceiling tiles, as well as under the cabinets to ensure higher light levels when required.

Infinity

The infinity lighting detail is inspired by James Turrell, one of the most influential artists of this century. This lighting detail is named after the illusion it creates—the seemingly endless appearance of a light filled void. The infinity is fundamentally a more advanced method of a slot or coffer. The razor edged finish reduces the apparent thickness of the ceiling to zero and the top of the detail, whether square, rectangular or round is always curved, eliminating any visual clues to the depth of the slot. The greater the scale, the more impact this technique has. The inclusion of colour allows for an infinite number of playful effects.

Above and opposite: To create the illusion of depth and wonder at the end of this private bar, an infinity detail is recessed into the super slim profile of the cantilevered ceiling. DMX controlled colour change LEDs are linked to a variety of additional effects including a backlit onyx panel, a delineated colour change floating ceiling and spotlit bar. The glazing above and beside, as well as the mirrored bar, multiplies the rainbow of hues as light bounces and reflects from one surface to another.

Infinity Detail

The infinity is an incredibly difficult detail to master on site. The quality of workmanship needs to be exemplary. Any rough plaster creates shadow and texture and will reduce the effect. Manufacturers provide pre-made razor edge profiles which assist enormously. Two colour temperatures or the use of RGB and white will heighten the effect, and create greater flexibility through the range of colours achieved. The greater the available depth in which to recess the lighting detail, the softer the effect. The infinity often looks more dramatic when set vertically into walls as opposed to horizontally (as shown) in ceilings.

Shelf Lighting

The key to successful shelf lighting is to ensure all reflections are minimised and there is complete concealment of the light source. This is often trickier than it looks. Highly polished veneers or the reflective surfaces of objects such as picture frames create reflections and refractions of light that often distract. A shelf when lit will provide additional interest to the room as well as strong focal points.

There are many alternatives to direct lighting from the front of the shelf—a softer version is to stop the shelf short at the back and backlight objects. Lights can be placed behind translucent material either horizontally or vertically. Lights can run vertically allowing for adjustable shelving or multiplied as in many high-end showrooms where they are lit from the back, side and the front.

Below: Linear LEDs set in to the top of the long recessed shelf draw one's attention to the depth of the space making if feel larger and more welcoming. Fittings set within wet areas will require a higher Ingress Protection to ensure there is no penetration of moisture. Many Linear LEDs are available as IP67, a suitably high protection for showers.

Opposite: The lit shelves provide a strong focal point to the study with the classic car collection and photos highlighted. Beautifully lit shelves provide a wonderful alternative to artwork.

Options for Shelf Lighting

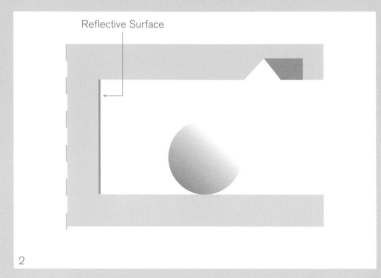

Reflective Surface

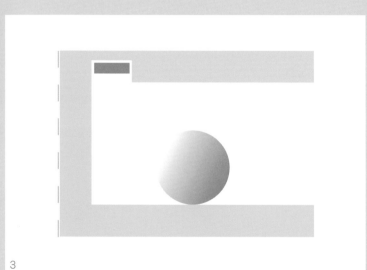

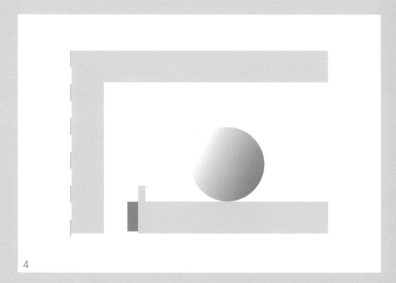

1. Basic shelf lighting with a small linear LED concealed behind a downstand. This works well until the shelves are sat too high above eye level and then one can often see the light source. Too large a downstand and the shelf becomes chunky. It is important to consider direct line of site and the size of downstand required.

2. A more advanced version of Detail 1 where an LED is set within a profile and recessed within the depth of the shelf. The joiner will router out a groove in advance. This detail also works well if you are using a mirrored or highly reflective back panel as the light source cannot be seen in the reflection.

3. Narrow shelves, particularly in bathrooms where hard materials are used to construct the details, work well with a single linear strip. The light source should be set in a deep profile so the LED cannot be seen.

4. To create a sense of depth, a slot is created at the back of the shelf to place the light source. This provides a very soft effect, gently silhouetting the objects. This is often used in conjunction with lighting from the front as well.

5

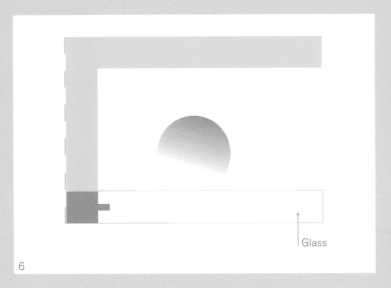

Glass

6

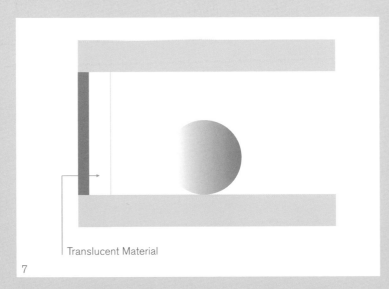

7

Translucent Material

6

5. Classic niche lighting, where a small LED downlight adds crisp sparkle to objects.

6. Edge lighting through glass or translucent material is very effective particularly when using colour—this is very popular in private bars.

7. Lighting through transparent materials such as Corian, marble or glass makes a stunning effect. Modern materials, such as prismatic Perspex make this a simple and effective technique. The effect is often greater when the back of a shelving unit is backlit, though this does place all objects in strong relief.

8. Placement of small lights on shelves adds interest. The enormous range of sculptural, illuminated objects create beautiful focal points.

Above: The shelving unit has recessed LEDs set at the back within a deep slot to provide a wash of light to the back of the very slim unit. This is to create the illusion of depth as well as to silhouette the small dark sculptures. (See Detail 4 on previous page).

Opposite: If adjustable shelves are used it is often easier to run the LEDs vertically and to set the shelves slightly short of the framework of the unit.

Backlighting and Silhouetting

To backlight or create a silhouette, there needs to be a distinct, directional light source from behind the object or material being lit. However, unless it is only the outline of the object that should be seen, additional lighting to the front will be required to accentuate tone, colour and texture. Backlighting of sculptures with simple shapes, or even trees within the garden can create dramatic effects as it emphasises the two-dimensional form of these three-dimensional works.

Edge lighting is the illumination of a material by running a light source along its edge. Traditionally, glass shelves were edge lit, however new materials have opened up a wealth of opportunity here. Prismatic Perspex (or acrylic) when lit from the side, ensures an even transmission of light across its surface, allowing even illumination of any material that sits upon it. This is often how we will create the effect of backlighting materials.

Above: A backlit ceiling panel imitates a skylight. Three colour temperature light sources were used—2,400k, 3,000k and 4,000k—to mimic the effects of daylight when colour tuned. With large expanses of glass, the volumes of light created from the light panel provide comfort by reducing the contrast in light levels when looking outside. A shadow gap harmonises with the softness of this detail and mirrors the colours available.

Opposite: The onyx floor is backlit using linear LED panels. It is essential to allow for access to drivers and panels as LEDs have been known to fail! Drivers are set within the kick plate of the central island for accessibility. The vertical wine racks have been spotlit along with the main front facing lower panel whilst the rest of the wine cellar requires the decorative pendant for general lighting.

Uplighting

Uplighting is complementary to many of the other lighting techniques. The critical detail is in the careful positioning of the fitting. If the light source sits too far from the wall it will not graze the surface, which is the most common mistake. If uncertain of distances from objects or surfaces being lit then use a sample fitting and test it on site.

Considerations when uplighting include output and beam width, the narrower the beam, the stronger the punch of light.

Above: A colour change LED uplight captures the elliptical stairs with a soft frame of light. A slot outlines the circular opening accentuating the lightness of the staircase as it reposes in space.

Opposite: Tiny recessed uplights set within the window frames draw the eye to the decorative plasterwork, which are further enhanced by small directional spotlights. Additional layers of light help to frame the kitchen creating a more intimate environment.

Any control gear required for the fitting will need to be placed in an accessible location. Drivers are often bigger than the cut-out of the fitting so will need to sit remotely. It is worth remembering that imperfect plasterwork or lack of attention from a decorator will all be highlighted as you graze a wall or surface with light.

Above: The architecture of the master bedroom suite is accentuated with the use of small LED uplights. These are discreetly spiked within the planter to create beautiful shadows, mounted to the beams to uplight into the pitched roof and set behind the bath to enhance the tiles. This dramatic circuit of light provides a wonderful ambience, enhancing the key features of the room.

Opposite: Uplights graze the decorative plaster wall highlighting and accentuating through the drama of shadows.

Spotlighting

Below: Surface-mounted spotlights attached to the beams are combined with recessed directional downlights set within the plastered ceiling. These are carefully placed quite close to the art as the ceilings are low, ensuring the art is optimally lit.

Opposite: The art is cross-lit with directional downlights beautifully enhancing the work and creating a focal point to the space.

Overleaf: The artwork showing Chairman Mao is lit with a framing projector, discreetly concealed within the ceiling. The secondary artwork framing the fireplace is only lit from the general light of the room.

Spotlights can be surface-mounted, track-mounted or fully recessed into the ceiling. Directional spotlights allow for precise control over which areas are lit. They can be used for highlighting specific accessories, furniture or artwork. Simple focus on artwork, or a narrow beam of light onto flowers or a fruit bowl is an effective way to create drama and impact.

The careful positioning of spotlights will ensure any glare is minimised—it is the effect of the light you wish to see not the source. Cowls, honeycomb lenses and louvres will be used to conceal the light source from view.

The angle of adjustability is essential to obtaining the correct position for lighting art. If the light source is too far away it will not be able to highlight the painting.

It is important to realise not all artwork needs to be spotlit. Art can look just as beautiful when lit from the glow of a table lamp or from the general light of a pendant. If too many pieces are spotlit then the eye does not know where to rest, and the room can appear busy. Less is often more.

Wall Washing

The intent of wall washing is to achieve uniform illumination on a vertical surface. The luminaire is placed on average one-quarter of the distance away from the surface with equal spacing between fittings. This effect eliminates scalloping which is the traditional effect of lighting a wall or artwork with directional downlights. The even illumination created from wall washers can be very useful if the position of an artwork is yet to be confirmed. Wall washing creates a bright, uniform wash of light, concealing imperfections by eliminating their shadows. Since there is an added emphasis to vertical surfaces, the eye tends to perceive a room with wall washers as larger and more spacious.

Below: Discreet asymmetric wall washers highlight both artwork and shelving units with a uniformly diffuse light. The effect is visually clean as wall washers reduce the typical scalloped effect of traditional downlights.

Wall Grazing

Wall grazing is similar to wall washing, however the light source is now located closer to the wall ensuring the light strikes the wall at a narrower angle. This effect works well on rough textured surfaces creating dramatic shadows and revealing subtleties that would otherwise be washed out with wall washing.

Left and below: Wall-mounted downlights graze the textured black granite wall revealing every fragment and indentation. The repetitive effect along the length of the surface creates a dramatic and contrasting interlude to the sanctuary of the pool.

Decorative Lighting

Below: Decorative lighting personalises the space as well as performing additional accent and general lighting.

Opposite: The Swarovski ceiling sparkles and dances providing a hypnotic and peaceful night-time effect. Tiny recessed uplights set within the window frame gently draw the eye to the window and the view beyond.

Decorative lighting, as opposed to technical or architectural lighting has a strong visual impact and therefore personalises a space. From the traditional glamour of a crystal chandelier to the high intensity, cool factor of a neon light. Decorative lighting is incredibly diverse. Clients often react strongly when shown various lights, often stating clearly what they don't like as opposed to a clear vision of what they do. From pendants, picture lights, wall sconces, neon and light sculptures, to the play of stars in a child's room, it is the distribution and intensity of the light source within a decorative fixture that must be highest up on the agenda when choosing a fitting. Although considered decorative, we are often reliant on these types of lights for our general or task lighting as well.

A large decorative item will have a huge impact on the appearance, atmosphere and overall look of a room. A decorative fixture may provide a historic, cultural or architectural reference and therefore its scale and finish will be of particular note.

As any decorative fixture is lit, it will by its nature often become the brightest point within the room, and therefore it is essential to check all the salient details before purchasing such as light output and distribution, lamp life, weight and whether it is dimmable. Very large or heavy chandeliers will require you to brace the ceiling to assist in weight distribution and to ensure a secure fixing.

Above: The pendant adds huge impact to the space and creates the drama required. The antique mirrored cupboards further enhance the effect. The tall bedside lamps frame the bed whilst tiny downlights create additional task light for reading and accenting artwork. Separate circuits allow flexibility with the layers of light ensuring the correct light levels for different times of the day.

Above: A sculptural pendant complements the diverse artwork. The subtle tones of the satin bronze framework mirror the detailing of the bespoke cabinets. The room is a masterpiece in restrained interior design allowing the pendant to take centre stage. Directional downlights highlight the art and boost light levels when task lighting is required.

Opposite: A glass pendant with complementary wall lights provides glamour and drama. Linear warm white LEDs set above the wardrobes assist in increasing the light levels and define the space. Additional wall lights frame the dressing table providing excellent task light for applying make-up. Light bounces and reflects off the mirrored cabinets and wardrobes creating a magically glamorous boudoir. Additional lighting in each wardrobe ensures all outfits, as well as a distinction between blues and blacks can be clearly seen.

Lighting Plans

The Client Brief

The success of a project often relies on the amount of time invested by the client. A clear brief, well illustrated with magazine tear-outs and inspirational images ensures nothing is forgotten or misunderstood. Common words such as 'bright', 'contemporary' and 'classic' do little to help convey to the lighting designer how the client feels about light. 'Brightness' is subjective, so it is worth breaking down the client's descriptions to ensure you have a clear understanding of their needs.

The kitchen shown here is partially set within a new conservatory and blessed with an abundance of natural light. The clients are creative and are avid cooks, and desired an open, informal space to entertain and enjoy. The lavishly planted garden plays a dominant role in the lighting scheme acting as a major focal point.

The clients' love of cooking, desire for colour and passion for their garden provided the structure for the lighting of their new kitchen and conservatory.

In trying to formalise the client brief you will often feel like an interrogator, asking a million questions in order to unpeel the layers of information required. Is the client left or right handed? This may determine the position of switches for ease of use. How much light do they need to do their tasks? Do they prefer darker, more intimate spaces, or are they happy to relax in a brighter room? Do they need a night light for an evening trip to the fridge? Do they cook together, entertain a lot—informally or formally? So many questions! However, each question is essential so that you can provide a lighting scheme that is suitable for their lifestyle.

It is worth noting all this information during the meeting so that it can be recalled, if required, at a later date.

Above and opposite: Garden lighting is critical when lighting a conservatory to ensure there is a clear view out at night. By increasing the volume of light outside the glazing and being able to reduce the internal lighting will ensure the view is not lost to the black mirror effect.

Previous: The high volumes of daylight provided through two skylights ensure the various materials used, their colours and texture are clearly seen.

Lighting Plans

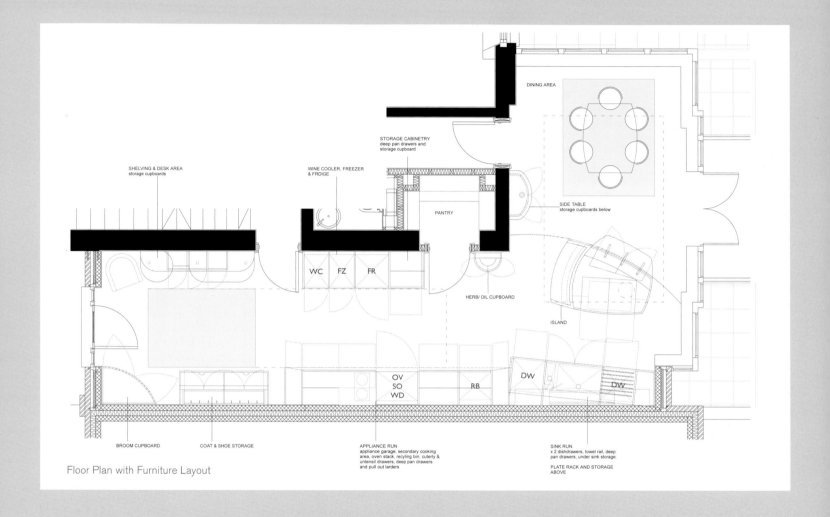

SHELVING & DESK AREA
storage cupboards

STORAGE CABINETRY
deep pan drawers and
storage cupboard

WINE COOLER, FREEZER
& FRDIGE

DINING AREA

SIDE TABLE
storage cupboards below

PANTRY

WC   FZ   FR

HERB/ OIL CUPBOARD

ISLAND

OV
SO
WD

RB

DW

DW

BROOM CUPBOARD

COAT & SHOE STORAGE

APPLIANCE RUN
appliance garage, secondary cooking
area, oven stack, recyling bin, cuterly &
untensil drawers, deep pan drawers
and pull out larders

SINK RUN
x 2 dishdrawers, towel rail, deep
pan drawers, under sink storage.

PLATE RACK AND STORAGE
ABOVE

Floor Plan with Furniture Layout

The starting point to a great lighting plan is an accurate floor plan. This will provide the base layer for furniture layouts as well all services including lighting, electrics, drainage and heating. A tape measure, scale ruler and careful attention to detail is required. If your plans have already been provided by an estate agent, architect or surveyor check them once carefully—inconsistencies easily arise. As a standard, architects draw floor plans at a scale of 1:50 with elevations at 1:20 or 1:25.

Once floor plans are in place, the next steps will be to markup a reflected ceiling plan and a scaled furniture layout. To assist, templates of furniture can often be downloaded from the Internet, make sure though they are to the same scale as to the one you are working to in your plan. Again, accuracy pays dividends.

Lighting schemes are often presented on general floor plans which means many of the ceiling details such as cornicing, beams and speakers are not represented. The benefit of a reflected ceiling plan is that it should highlight details and restrictions that appear in the ceiling which might affect the installation of any lights.

A reflected ceiling plan (RCP) will clearly show changes in level, skylights, voids, sloping soffits, air conditioning units, hatches, cornices, ceiling roses, steels and vents. Unless you are using detailed architectural plans, with clear sections and elevations, it is surprising how often details on the ceiling are missed altogether, particularly around staircases and in attics and basements. It is important to note as soon as possible the ceiling construction, position of joists, pipes and ductwork as this will all have considerable impact on your lighting plan.

When creating your lighting plan the easiest way to start is by shading onto your floor plan areas that require dedicated task lighting. Once this is complete consider any major decorative lighting fixtures such as pendants and shade these in as well. Accent lighting can be represented as yellow lines against the wall where artwork is lit. Once the shading is completed you will start to have a clear picture as to how your lighting is currently balanced. This is when you may wish to look at filling in the voids, if required with further lighting.

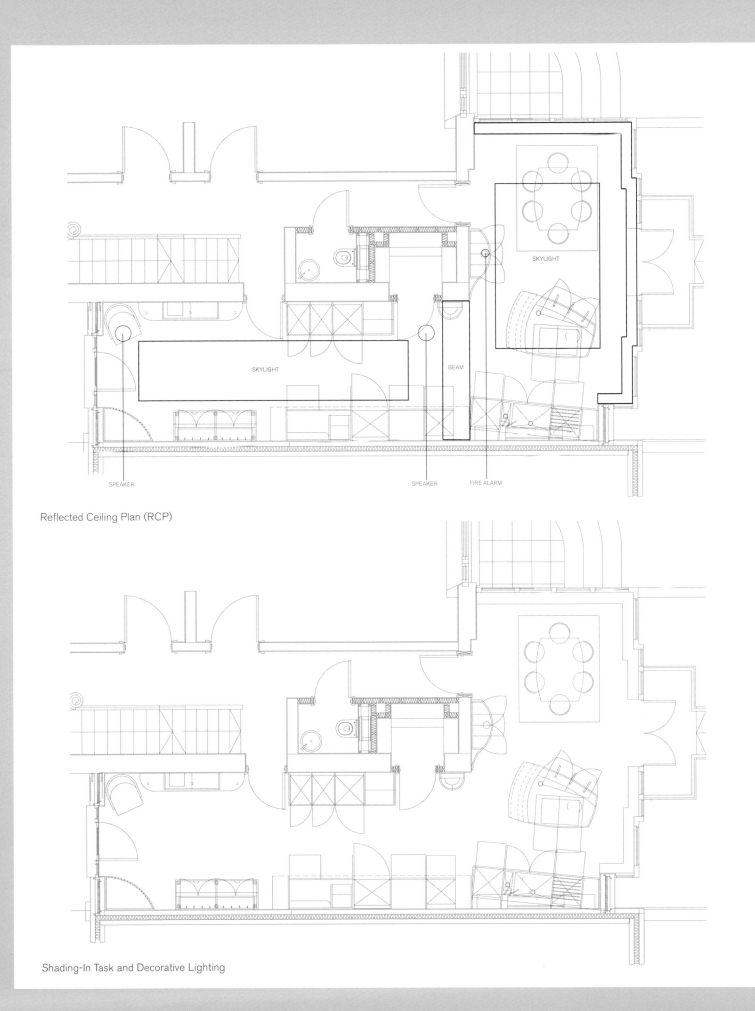

Reflected Ceiling Plan (RCP)

SPEAKER   SPEAKER   FIRE ALARM

SKYLIGHT

SKYLIGHT

BEAM

Shading-In Task and Decorative Lighting

Opposite: The illustrations show two different ways to circuit a lighting plan. Depending on the size of the job, or the number of circuits specified you may start to prefer one method over another. For more complicated lighting plans with multiple circuits, referencing each fitting is often clearer, however, having the bubble lines linked to each fitting on the same circuit would be the more traditional approach.

Hand drawn elevations with yellow pencil shading to represent the indicative position of the lighting.

With the elevations and perspective drawings completed you then highlight the areas with yellow pencil where the lighting will have the greatest impact. This will assist enormously in conveying the lighting effects you are trying to achieve. Slowly your lighting plan will take shape. Luckily, it is not rocket science! It just takes time and careful consideration as to how you will use the space. More often than not, lighting plans are rushed within a generic layout for tender documentation and this remains until the electrician starts to query positions at first fix.

On lighting plans draw the light fittings to scale unless they are too tiny to be read, allowing you to see their impact in the space. This is particularly important with pendants on plans and wall lights on elevations. Once the lighting plan is further developed you will need to specify precise dimensions, such as the distance from wall or height of wall light. Electricians rarely use scale rulers.

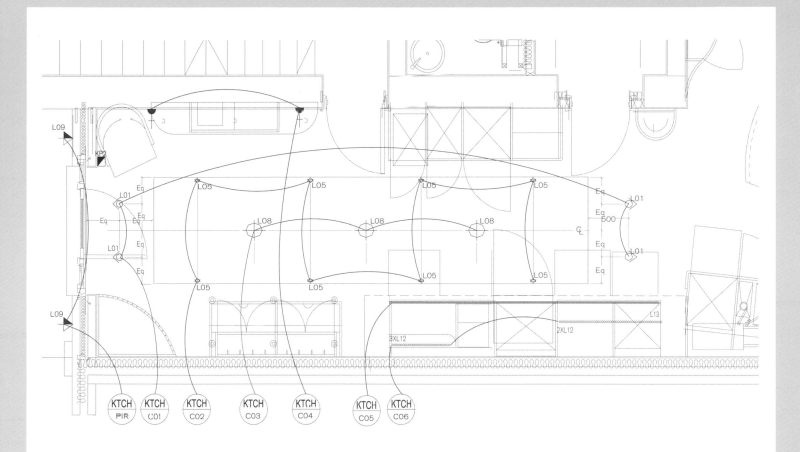

Traditional lighting plan: Each fitting on the same circuit is linked together with bubble lines.

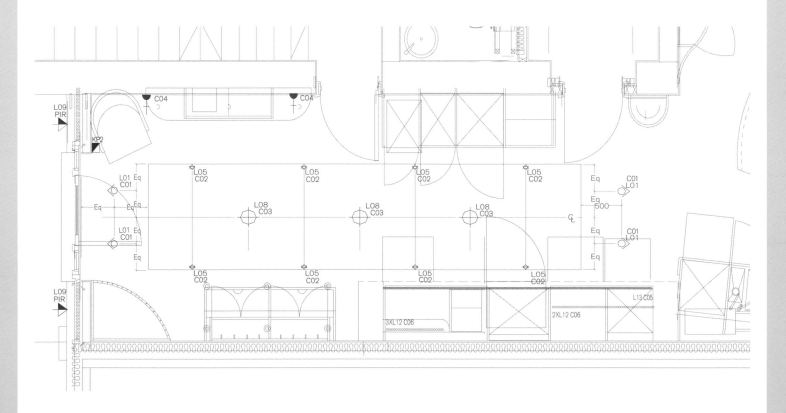

Alternative lighting plan: Each light fitting has a product and circuit reference next to it illustrating how it is to be circuited.

	L01	LED Directional Downlights CR190+ 7W GU10 38° 2700K
	L02	Credo ARIII, 12v 100W Surface Spot
	L03	OMITTED in revision A
•	L04	LD42 1.2W 350mA 12° 2950K UPLIGHT
	L05	Elin IW 350mA Small Warm White STARPOINT
	L06	Undershelf Eyelid LED 4W 500mA
	L07	Medium Decorative Pendant
	L08	Small Decorative Pendant
	L09	Exterior Decorative Wall Lights
	L10	LED Light Tape Slots 12V 5W/m 2700k
-XXXXX-	L11	OMITTED
-OOOO-	L12	LED Light Tape 12V 10W/m 2700K
	L13	LED Light Sheet 12V Double-sided 3700K
	L14	Small Pendant Task light

Electrical Legend

	5Amp wall socket
5	5Amp floor socket
X	Supply for future lighting
	Lutron Homeworks Control Plate
MU	OMMITED
SBE	Supply by electrician
E	Emergency
Cxx	Circuit Specification
	LED Drivers
Cxx	Switch
	Speaker

light.iQ
LONDON

Client Name:
Site Address:

Drawing:

Stage:	Issue Date:	Checked By:	Scale:

Designer: Rebecca Weir

The lighting key/legend shows the symbols, with reference number and description.
The title block includes essential contact details, revisions and scale.

Circuits illustrate how the scheme will be operated, and every circuit requires a switch, PIR or photocell to operate it. Switch plates should be carefully positioned on site accommodating the flow of traffic. It can be useful to markup on site where you will want to switch certain lights on from, as in many cases the same lights will be switched on from more than one location. As the lighting designer you are responsible for selecting the architectural light fittings. Each product chosen will need to be referenced on the plan and will require a product specification sheet which will include the following information: manufacturer's contact details and part code, voltage and wattage, IP rating, recommended driver or transformer, CRI, lumen output, and any additional accessories such as lenses or louvres.

A key, normally situated top right of the plan, will clarify what each symbol used on the plan is. Sitting below and bottom right is the title block. This should include your contact details, client information, area specified, date of plan and subsequent revisions.

When designing a space there is often a key deciding factor—the love of a particular pendant, a great piece of art or furniture. Once this is placed on the plan then multiple layers of light are built around it. With no fixed rules you may wish to consider either your general, accent, task or decorative lighting first. Slowly as these are sketched on it is easier to see other areas that require further lighting.

Each genre of lighting would benefit from its own circuit, this creates plenty of flexibility. However, if you use too many circuits, a client can become bewildered by buttons. Specify no more than four switches in any one location because even the most brilliant of minds forgets which switch does what. Or look to technology to assist and utilise pre-set control systems for ease of use and their energy saving benefits.

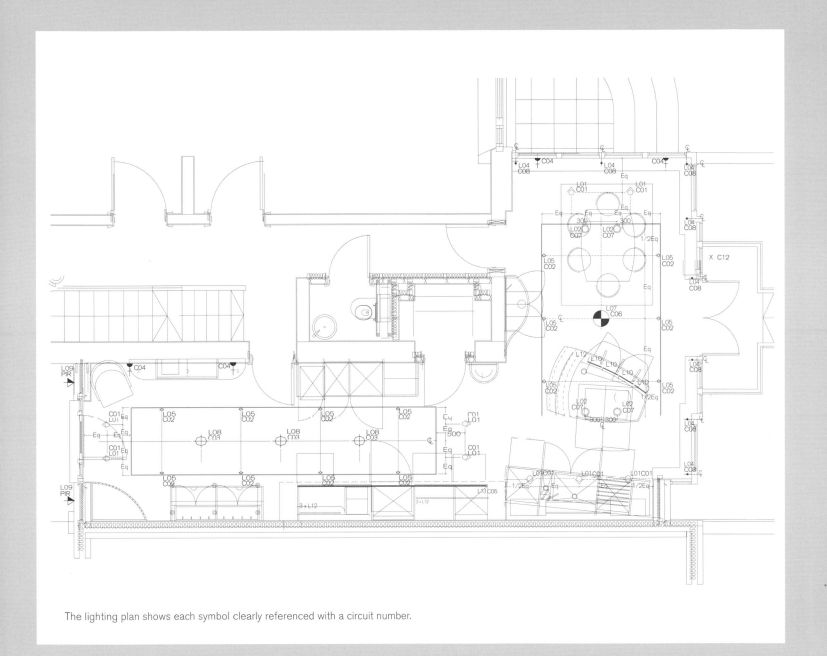

The lighting plan shows each symbol clearly referenced with a circuit number.

The plan illustrates:

Circuit one: General and task lighting from directional downlights.

Circuit two: Swarovski LED crystals set centred within the upstand of the skylights for sparkle.

Circuit three: Three pendants set centred within the skylight providing colour and ambience.

Circuit four: 5-amp sockets for lamps.

Circuit five: Backlighting the Corian cupboard unit.

Circuit six: Pendant set centred in main conservatory.

Circuit seven: Task lights surface-mounted to upstand of conservatory for superb lighting for the dining table and island.

Circuit eight: Miniature LEDs uplight the window reveals creating a framework of light to the view.

Cupboard Lighting is linked to door operated switches. A centralised home automation system provides control to all circuits via 'scenes' of light operated through keypad, remote or phone.

The small LED uplights set within the window ledges frame the view drawing the eye to the lush garden beyond. Linked to this are layers of low level light ensuring that at dusk, with little other distractions, there is a gentle focus on the garden. Two layers of linear LEDs were mounted under the breakfast bar accentuating the textural concrete and providing additional task lighting to the island work top.

Building upon our first layer of light was the second consideration, and with so much glazing it was essential to ensure excellent task lighting for the main work surfaces. This was achieved through cabinet lights recessed in the shelf above the sink as well as adjustable spotlights sat within the upstand of the conservatory.

A softer and more decorative ambience is achieved through the specification of a chandelier. This is set centred within the conservatory ensuring a warm volume of light reaches the entire room.

As we age, dedicated task lighting for reading and preparing food becomes a greater priority. To ensure high comfort levels additional task lights were centred above the dining table so the morning paper could be read comfortably. The position of the lights also ensures that when food is brought to the table it is highlighted, and all the colours and textures sing.

Above: Linear LEDs set within the island accentuate the variety of textured finishes.

Opposite: Backlit Corian cupboards create a soft framework to the unit creating a dramatic interlude to the artisan space.

The clients and renowned experimental kitchen designer Johnny Grey agreed to push the design further with the use of backlit Corian cupboards. Multiple mock-ups and samples were required to ensure the optimum effect which is both striking and pleasing to the eye. The backlit unit frames the space and creates a dramatic focal point. The backlit unit when turned onto full light ensures there is never a dull day, however, as dusk settles, the gentlest dimmed light allows it to resonate quietly, ensuring its translucency is not lost to the darkness.

Colourful pendants, complementing the hand painted furniture lift the space and draw our attention to the scale and volume of the architecture.

A little extra sparkle materialises with the small crystal LEDs mounted into the upstand of the roof light. This magic prevents the glazing from becoming a dark void after dusk.

Finally, with eight circuits, either individually controlled or built into scenes, there is maximum flexibility and a lifetime of choice. The pre-set control system at its simplest ensures three scenes: off, raise and lower. Due to the high natural light levels these will vary tremendously throughout the seasons so instructions on simple, manual adjustments should always be provided. During winter, a morning scene will require greater volumes of artificial light than at the same time during summer. In many homes, this would not be quite so significant as levels of daylight would be more moderate.

In summary: a unique scheme for a wonderful client and designer, demanding in detail at times, but outstanding in results.

Above and opposite: The photographs show the backlit Corian unit. The top right image is a close up cross section of the cupboard door.

Case Studies

Entrance Halls

The entrance hall is often the first impression to your home. Creating an inviting space provides warmth and comfort for your guests. Decorative items such as lanterns, wall lights and pendants set the tone. However, it is often concealed architectural lights, such as downlights, discreetly placed, that are doing much of the work to help lift light levels and lead the eye from room to room. For example, in the opposite photo, the recessed directional downlights highlighting the art also provide good reflected light into the room. The small recessed floor uplights accentuate the architecture and frame the central pendant with light.

Previous: Shadow gaps in the shower and steam room, along with underlighting of benches mirror each other creating visual harmony in their symmetry.

Opposite: The shape of the wall lights complement the structural opening whilst the candle's effect is warm and welcoming. The small 2W LED uplights, set in the window accentuate the architecture and draw you in to enjoy the view and the garden beyond.

First Impressions Count

Key considerations in hallways include the amount of available daylight, the position and number of focal points—whether artwork, sculpture or the architecture. Decorative pieces, whether furniture, wall finishes, artwork or lighting personalise the space. A trick in traditional dark hallways is to place downlights on either side of a lantern, creating a focus on the historic or decorative references whilst allowing the recessed lights to provide most of the light.

Layers of light will create interest and flexibility. A classic example of this is a central lantern framed by table lamps on a console table. Two layers ideally on different circuits provide various light levels when required.

Left: The central pendant creates a strong focal point to the space. The open lamps offer generous light levels highlighting the architectural detailing of the ceiling. Good light levels in the centre of the room are important to ensure the room does not appear flat as there are large volumes of daylight entering from the windows at either end.

Opposite top: The antique mirror, opposite the front door, reflects the available daylight, whilst downlights create quiet pools of light allowing the sculptural pedestal to focus our attention.

Opposite bottom: The artwork is beautifully lit with a series of recessed directional downlights. Halogen lamps are used to ensure perfect colour rendering.

Contemporary Kitchen and Pool Extension

This contemporary family living space is dominated by incredible vistas to the garden and large volumes of natural light.

The pool, sat beyond the glass doors of the kitchen, offers a unique visual experience as the space transforms into a dynamic piece of lit art.

Teamwork is essential to the success of a project. It takes confidence and patience by all parties to realise complex schemes.

Previous: The exterior wall lights are mounted higher than normal to ensure the view internally from the garden is less interrupted by patterns of light. Their function to cast light both onto the terrace as well as upwards, catching the frame of the iroko architecture, ensure their form is appropriate to the requirement.

Opposite: The family room remains alive and welcoming as the patterns of daylight transform the space with shafts of light and playful shadows.

The kitchen incorporates a range of light effects. A shadow gap, set above the AGA cooker (at the far end of the room) conceals powerful downlights providing excellent task lighting to the workspace. Linear lighting is also used within the shadow gap and under the breakfast bar creating a softer alternative effect used most often at night.

When used as general lights the downlights are kept symmetrical to the architecture. When the downlights are used as dedicated task lights then their placement is related to the task at hand. For example, over the dining table, where homework and a multitude of other activities take place, the downlights are centred over the table and not within the flat ceiling space.

Below: Concealed within the shadow gap is a series of downlights centred on each of the wood veneered cupboard units. These downlights accentuate their grain and texture whilst also providing additional reflected light to the room. The linear LED light, set within the shadow gap as a second circuit provides a soft, diffused light which complements the lighting set under the breakfast bar and the island. These two layers work in harmony and allow one to read the entire length and volume of the room.

Opposite: The directional downlights accenting the art provide further balance and a strong focal point. Recessed light slots set within the skylights prevent this from falling into obscurity at night.

Left: The raise and lower floor provided a multitude of challenges. Customised light fittings were designed without bezels to ensure the floor moved seamlessly. Once the floor is down, the rope is hooked for the children to have a swinging time.

Opposite: The functional lighting is provided by both concealed lights within the shadow gaps framing the pool as well as by downlights over the walkway. This ensured the ceiling is kept as clutter free as possible to minimise distractions away from the architecture.

From pilates to parties, swimming activities to lazy summer days. This multifunctional pool room with its raise and lower floor is used daily. The lighting design needed to incorporate various demands from a morning workout to the energetic excitement of a children's birthday party.

Why do two colours, put one next to the other, sing?
Can one really explain this?
No. Just as one can never learn to paint.

Pablo Picasso

Personalising Light

The swimming pool provided a unique opportunity to personalise the space with a customised piece of lit art. This took the form of a saying from one of the clients' favourite songs "All these things that we've done". The quote was converted into Braille which was then mapped onto the mother of pearl mosaic wall. Fibre-optic light points were used to create this effect. When switched on, the phrase appears in sparkling form creating a dynamic message which can change colour to suit the family's mood. The glistening reflection of the pool and glazing provides a magical ambience.

Below and opposite: Edge lit fibre-optics set within a resin filled channel delineates the edge of the pool. With a colour wheel providing a multitude of colours this plays against the hues of the fibre-optic spotlights grazing the base of the pool.

The shadow gaps within the pool conceal linear wall washers which graze the surfaces with both coloured and white light. The pool has a multitude of effects on different circuits ensuring there is never a dull day. A DMX control system was utilised too, accessed via wall stations and iPads to ensure the client has easy access to change the dynamics of the room as desired. From rainbows to ribbons of colour, there is never a dull moment.

The exterior lighting utilises several circuits from a dedicated lamp sat over the exterior dining table to linear patterns of colour linking the drama of the internal lighting scheme. The greatest volume of light comes from a moonlighter, set high within a tree providing dappled patterns of light to the lawn.

Overleaf: Rainbows of colour fill the pool creating a dynamic space. Complemented by the recessed linear exterior profiles, a kaleidoscope of colour awaits.

Think of what starlight
And lamplight would lack
Diamonds and fireflies
If they couldn't lean against Black.

Mary O'Neill, *Hailstones and Halibut Bones*

Gym

The converted barn provides a contemporary family gym. Plentiful natural light through both lower and higher level glazing creates a dynamic space perfect for an energising work out. The high levels of daylight ensure that the artificial light is only really required from dusk creating a very efficient lighting scheme. Artichoke Pendants, a classic design masterpiece by Poul Henningsen, fill the voids with diffuse reflected light.

Four layers of light accentuate the architecture. The first layer is small LED uplights set close to the vertical supports, and the second is a linear LED mounted into a small recess detail to accentuate the length of the room and uplight the pitch. Thirdly, small LEDs discreetly mounted to the beams uplight the vaults highlighting the framework and texture of the wood. The fourth layer, providing strong focal points and generous volumes of light are the three pendants.

It is essential in such a minimal scheme with exposed elements to consider the position of all control gear in advance. Drivers will need to be accessible for future maintenance yet discreetly located. Electricians often prefer to house all control gear in one cupboard, and with long distances care must be taken to prevent voltage drop between fitting and driver resulting in loss of power and light output. It is the electrician's responsibility to calculate these distances and the size of cables required to minimise any impact.

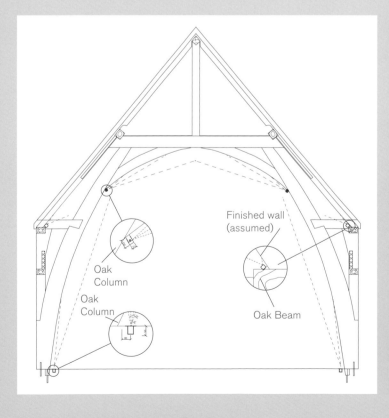

Gym Detail

Fittings on an adjustable bracket are fixed to the junction between the oak column and arch. The final position is to be adjusted on site to achieve the best lighting effect. Asymmetrical LEDs set in the floor uplight the arches. The lens is tilted six degrees away from the beam, and the 25 degree optic follows the curve of the oak column.

A linear LED set above the oak beam provides a wash of light to the pitched room. The profile in which the LED sits should be positioned at an angle so that the light output is parallel to the illuminated surface.

Finished wall
(assumed)

Oak
Column

Oak
Column

Oak Beam

Pool Pavilions

The bold entrance sets the mood to the pool pavilion as a fun, dynamic space for the family. Bespoke furniture is carefully integrated providing key focal points. The pavilion is discreetly tucked into the woodland setting and benefits from interlinking ponds, connecting the internal and external elements.

Left and below: Daylight dances through the leaves, creating playful patterns whilst energising the ground below.

Opposite: The entrance is as dramatic as the pool with deep hues, playful pendants and a striking backlit corona bench setting the scene.

Above: The ceiling is kept clear of downlights, only to be punctuated by a hanging garden of fibre-optic tails which dance in the wind. The success of the fibre-optics lies in the use of a sparkle wheel which creates magical twinkles and movement. This hypnotic effect is akin to the dance of a flame.

Above: The linear lighting is recessed between the original beams. This provides good volumes of general light and accentuates the linear framework of the space. The glazed art panels, backlit with daylight benefit from being artificially lit at night.

We eat light, drink it in through our skins.
With a little more exposure to light, you feel part
of things physically. I like feeling the power of light
and spaces physically because then you can order it
materially. Seeing is a very sensuous act—there's a
sweet deliciousness to feeling yourself see something.

James Turrell

Above: Lighting is carefully integrated within the
joinery, highlighting its shape and providing task
lighting. The bespoke Corian shelves are backlit with
an LED light sheet. This customised material enables
the magnificent translucent forms.

Opposite: Decorative pendants frame the bar, the
complementing colours link through to the decorative
glazed artwork.

Opposite and above: The pond acts as a reflective tool accentuating the drama of the pavilion as it glows like a lantern at night. A little colour enhances the interior scheme and provides a fun addition for the children.

Overleaf: The vertical panels of light are dimmed to such a low light output that they start to look like a paint effect. An extremely subtle palette of colours can be created, so subtle they look like nothing more than a blushing shadow.

Living Room

There was an opportunity to provide a dynamic living room within this open loft space. The raw and majestic steel framework beckoned for attention. The form of the space is emphasised by the lighting which is set within the original framework. At the touch of a button colours can change and chase one another creating multiple effects. The lighting can mimic sunrise to sunset and every shadow and permutation in between. Accent lighting on artwork, card and dining tables is separately circuited to allow maximum flexibility.

Due to the inconsistencies of the original beams the installation tested the patience of a saint. Each one was carefully measured as subtle variations in widths and depths between them would have caused inappropriate light spill. An edge lit prismatic acrylic panel was used with RGB linear LEDs running on one side and warm white 2,500k on the other. This allowed for us to create the warmth required for the client as well as the additional flexibility of colour. Custom products require long timescales with 25 days allowed for this installation. These need to be carefully integrated into the project diary to ensure deadlines are met. The ability to dim to very low light levels was critical due to the highly mirrored surfaces within the room.

Opposite: The warmth of the generous fireplace is accentuated by the soft hues of the lighting scheme.

Colour is the place where the mind
and the universe meet.

Paul Cezanne

Above: Colour in all its brilliance and variety changes our response to the room immediately. A subtle change in tone can create a strong emotional response from us. Flexibility and variety are often key to keeping a family content.

Opposite: Table and free standing lamps, sculptural in form, provide a decorative addition to the space. This is an important layer of warm light which creates a more intimate welcome.

Exteriors

Exterior lighting provides a feeling of safety and reassurance, an essential emotional connection to your home. Creating a strong first impression will provide enjoyment as you return home after a long day. A beautifully lit drive and front door creates a fabulous welcome drawing you into the comfort of what lies beyond.

Facade lighting, whether illuminating the whole building or architectural elements, such as columns or pediments, should be addressed separately to security lighting. Security specialists should advise on deterrent lighting, however, ensure an override switch is easily accessible so the floodlights can be switched off and not triggered by guests when entertaining. Several exterior circuits will ensure you keep the lighting to your home subtle and in tune with the occasion, allowing differing accents for varying times of the year.

Garden lighting, most importantly, will transform an exterior space. The garden should be treated as a jewel, something precious, to be treasured. All the rules which apply to lighting the interior of a home apply to the exterior. Multiple layers, plentiful circuits, strong focal points, great task lighting and good ambience will ensure plenty of delights throughout the seasons. Colour temperature, colour rendering and light output will all need to be considered when selecting products. If a colour temperature that is too warm is used, the garden becomes an amber wash of foliage, however, too cool and a ghostly air prevails. Most designers stick with 3,000k, with slight adjustments if moonlighting (cooler), or warmer if accenting brick or honey coloured stone.

Above: The uplighting of the wall catches the sail overhead providing gentle reflected light to the seating space. Additional spotlights discreetly set behind rocky outcrops flood the planting beyond creating a strong focal point to the back of the garden.

Opposite left: The bronze lantern provides an architectural reference, the up/down wall lights frame the front door adding drama and reinforcing the symmetry. The floor mounted candle lanterns are introduced to generate further warmth and sparkle on arrival.

Opposite right: The captivating flames of the candle lanterns highlight the glistening brilliance of the uplit fountains. The dynamic movement and energy of both water and fire work in harmony with the four central spiritual elements considered as the essential basis to any garden—earth, air, fire and water.

The 'Black Mirror Effect'

The 'black mirror' is described as the moment you start to see your own reflection when looking out through glass. The dark reflected effect of the glazing creates a harsh internal environment as the windows effectively become walls of polished black mirror. To rectify this you need to be able to dim your internal lights so they are at a lower output than the light level outside and install exterior lighting.

Integrating lighting into a brise soleil or onto the facade of your home helps enormously as large volumes of light are introduced immediately outside the glazing creating a portal in which to view the garden beyond.

Above and opposite: Lighting within the brise soleil and extended canopy, as well as controlled lighting internally ensures we break through the black mirror effect allowing you to view the garden beyond. The soft general light to the surrounding features, including the steps, watermill and textured brick walls ensure focal points immediately outside of the house providing a connection to the landscape. In larger gardens, we often use fewer light fittings the further you move away from the house ensuring critical pathways and focal points are lit.

Focal Points

In larger gardens one or two focal points suffice, from water features, sculptures or significant trees to wrapping or hanging light sculptures within spaces. There are large numbers of decorative light fixtures now available, from exterior chandeliers and fairy lights to innovative light art that compete for your attention. Again, restraint pays dividends. Allow for the addition of decorative lights by installing switched outlets in the garden. This will ensure you can develop the scheme as time and budget allows.

Above: The old oak tree dominates the garden with its broad canopy. The gnarled trunk is uplit revealing its beautifully aged form. The bench beneath is caught by the Moonlighter, a discreet light fitting set high in the branches above throwing a stunning dappled pattern of light onto the landscape below.

Opposite: Evenly lit from all sides, the fountain becomes the central focal point to the wider landscape. A sculpture carefully placed at the end of the path creates intrigue for the spaces that lie beyond.

Fireplaces and Lanterns

We are drawn to fire, as moths are drawn to the light. The magic and dance of the flame draws us closer as our primal responses are heightened. We respond at a physiological level to the movement of light, whether it is clouds passing over on a sunny day, the flash of lightning, the chaos of a fairground or the flicker of candle and fire light. It is this innate, emotional response we need to meet when designing the lighting of a garden.

Above: The circular firepit draws the family into the depths of the garden; a perfect spot to gather and enjoy sunset. The uplit pleached trees create privacy whilst abundant foliage ensures total immersion into the scents of the garden.

Opposite: A contemporary fireplace takes centre stage in this urban garden. Framed with lanterns and candles either side as well as additional ones placed on columns along the length of the garden, it is a magical and intimate place.

Below: The outdoor pavilion provides hours of fun for all the family. Great task lighting for barbecuing is provided by small recessed downlights set within the wooden canopy and a huge firepit for teenagers creates an intimate and social place to gather round and enjoy. The surface-mounted directional wall lights graze the textured brickwork whilst candle lanterns frame the seating space.

The multiple layers of light, from uplights to pleached trees and moonlight on the lawn, ensure plenty of flexibility. The magic of the twilight hour draws us outside as the dance and energy of the night creates a new picture in the landscape for us to enjoy.

Above: The magnificent magnolia tree is enhanced by a series of tiny uplights ensuring the full canopy is lit. With an entertainment area below, task lighting has been introduced by mounting a series of small spotlights onto the branches which highlight the dining area beneath.

Left: The formality of the garden is accentuated by the symmetry of the uplit trees. A moonlighter set into a mature tree at the back of the garden provides an incredibly subtle wash of light preventing the garden from sitting in complete darkness at night.

Opposite: A moonlight softly accentuates the immediate planting within the small garden. The gentle underlighting of the bench invites you to enjoy the change in seasons.

Moonlighting

Moonlighting is a favourite lighting technique. Place a powerful light source high up (often 4–6m), strapped to a branch or trunk of the tree and then light down through the branches. The result is a diffuse wash of patterned light which creates dappled shadows from the leaves and branches below the source. By using a wide beam of light the effect is very natural. A benefit of this soft, diffuse wash of light to the landscape is that it helps to allow other lighting to subtly feature as the contrast of what is lit is reduced.

Step Lighting

Step lights are an easy way to introduce a little drama. Without fail they look dramatic, always drawing the viewer to a space beyond. It is essential to use a low glare fitting, one with a cowl if there is direct line of sight. If you have very long narrow steps you may wish to use a narrower beam, however broad steps may benefit from greater coverage and therefore a wider beam.

In settings where there is no light pollution it is essential to light both the first and last step for safety.

Left: Step lights are mounted to the tread as there is no string to recess a light into.

Opposite top right: Lighting every third tread ensures the effect is more dramatic, as the light is read in relation to the shadows created.

Opposite top left: The light coloured stone allows the light to reflect and travel further along their length. Very wide steps will need fittings at each end.

Opposite below: LED step lights are recessed into the wall with a close offset to the tread ensuring a dramatic and visible beam of light to the surface.

Colour in the Garden

The introduction of colour provides hours of fun and lifts spirits. Various hues work beautifully in contemporary settings. However, coloured lights and foliage will provide very mixed results!

An alternative to using coloured lights is to introduce a complementary palette of colours to enhance the architecture. Contemporary greys and blacks, although seemingly very brave, offset the foliage magnificently.

But as they say—beauty lies in the eye of the beholder.

Below left: A fun roof garden with splashes of colour set within a dense urban environment. Low level lighting ensures the view of the rooftops beyond remains uninterrupted.

Below right: The deep grey trellising provides an intimate backdrop to the luxury of the hot tub.

Opposite: RGB linear LED strips are recessed within the architecture to frame the spaces. RGB uplights set beneath the opaque planters complement the linear detailing.

Roof Terraces

Roof terraces often require more light per square metre due to the high amount of light pollution and lighting from surrounding houses. Strong focal points are required to draw you into the space. Low level lighting, set beneath planters and benches prevent obstruction of the view beyond.

Left and below: The generous roof garden with far reaching views of the city gains new life at night. As dusk beckons, discreet lighting re-energises the garden drawing our attention to new spaces and different aspects. Small crystal uplights set within the decking draw you to the end of the terrace and lead you to the soft underlighting of the seating. Surface-mounted downlights accentuate the pergoda and illuminate the planting below. The final layer of lighting is the soft uplighting of the olive trees gently framing the space and creating a sense of intimacy when required.

Opposite: The tiny roof garden with high retaining walls is viewed as a piece of art through the picture window. Blue backlight, shadow, contrast and a generous use of mirrors creates interest and the illusion of depth.

Internal Courtyards

Internal courtyards are a wonderful addition to basements creating further contact to the outside world. These bijou spaces need to be carefully lit to draw the eye through the glazing. High light levels can easily be obtained by discreetly placing floodlights out of the line of sight above windows and doors. These will provide a volume of light negating internal reflections.

Left, below and opposite: To create a connection to the main garden, low level lights draw the eye up the stairs. These discreet fittings provide a connection with the internal step lights leading to the lower basement. Linear light recessed at a high level in the window frames the view.

Water Features

Water features provide a new dimension to any garden from the soft sound of falling water, to the movement and reflection that is created. On occasion, a water feature might be left without internal lighting to create dramatic imagery on the still surface. Water features need to be carefully maintained so that you are not highlighting moss and algae.

Above: The water feature is lit with pond lights discreetly set beneath the decked bridges so that the effect of the light is seen but not the source. For additional drama the specimen trees are accentuated whilst leaving the foliage between in the shadows.

Opposite: The temple is lit allowing it to reflect on the still pond, and the surrounding foliage is emphasised delineating the water for safety as well as beauty.

Outdoor Dining

Task lighting is essential to ensure safety in any exterior cooking space. A directional wall or surface-mounted spotlight, which can be locally switched on and off will work well. The lighting for outdoor tables is often trickier to manage as they may be placed away from any supporting structures from which you can light. Although candles work well, they are often not enough on their own. Decorative rechargeable table lanterns are popular as well as free-standing exterior lamps that provide diffused light over the table. There are also many parasols which have lighting and heating incorporated creating soft, warm cocooned spaces.

Above and opposite: The courtyard garden benefits from multiple layers of light. A directional wall mounted spotlight provides excellent task lighting, and linear LEDs set beneath the exterior dining bar highlight its solidity and form. Equally spaced uplights accentuate the trellis and provide delineation to the space. They also catch the underside of the umbrella ensuring good reflected light. The Japanese influence is felt through the uplit bamboo and the backlit trellised screen creating great volumes of light when entering at night.

Implementation and Installation

An electrician experienced with exterior installations is required, as the weather and local wildlife will soon highlight any inherent weaknesses in the scheme. It is worth detailing at the outset of the project how cables are to be run and where any junction boxes or connections are to be made, ensuring they remain out of line of sight. There are many options in which to control your garden with excellent wireless solutions if switching has not been accommodated for internal use. It is good practice to ensure all your external lighting is linked to a photocell and timer so that they are not left on during daylight hours. A photocell will bring your lights on at dusk for a designated time ensuring that as you arrive home the garden or drive is beautifully lit.

Above left: Moonlighters are particularly tricky to install. You will require very tall ladders or a cherry picker and a very willing electrician. Note that during installation it is worth mentioning how critical the position of the fitting is to light through the branches to the landscape below, otherwise the installer will be revisiting the top of the tree to reposition the light again soon.

Above right: Lights centrally placed within the garden, whether fixed in shingle, lawn or flower beds should ideally be recessed. This ensures they remain as discreet as possible and are not disturbed by children, pets or your gardener.

Opposite: A stunning exterior chandelier creates a magical adornment to any tree. Hung in odd numbers and at different heights, they allow for an enchanting story to unfold.

Inspiration

Light Artists

James Turrell

James Turrell has secured a place in the contemporary art scene as one of the most innovative and acclaimed artists experimenting with the possibilities of light and space in art. Turrell's works, often using bright colour, create singular visual experiences, whilst at the same time influencing sensory perceptions. For the onlooker, his works can provide a near spiritual experience. While completing his Bachelor of Arts degree at Pomona College in southern California, Turrell examined not only perceptual psychology—his academic emphasis—but also a broader array of topics. His early interest in subjects as varied as geology, astronomy and mathematics intimates the versatility his artistic production embodies. In his art, the synthesis of seemingly disparate spheres becomes apparent.

Olafur Eliasson (below)

One of the most prominent Scandinavian artists in the contemporary art scene, Olafur Eliasson, produces large-scale installations that use elemental materials to enhance unique experiences for the viewer. His works often utilise water and temperature to produce their unique conditions, but a uniting concern is light. In his 2010 installation *Your Blind Passenger*, light is attenuated in order to play with perceptions of space and perspective. Well known works include the 2008 man-made waterfalls, the *New York City Waterfalls*, and the *Green River* series where he introduced an environmentally safe dye into rivers in various cities from 1998–2001.

Carlos Cruz-Diez (above)

Venezuelan artist Carlos Cruz-Diez is a kinetic and op artist who creates vibrant, colourful works that explore perception using colour and line. Cruz-Diez draws upon various sources of inspiration in his work such as the works of Josef Albers and George Seurat who inform Cruz-Diez's engagement with colour. The differences between European and Venezuelan flora also shapes his practice. Concentrating on colour and line, he actively engages the viewer through using changes in movement and an awareness of perception.

Anthony McCall (right)

Now known for his 'solid light' productions and his exploration of the similarities between light and sculpture, artist Anthony McCall first gained recognition through his involvement with the London Film-makers' Co-op. During his time with the group in the early 1970s, McCall experimented with fire in film performances, a practice that carried on into his later career. In 1973, McCall relocated to New York, and produced his first 'solid light' film, *Line Describing a Cone*. It was at this time that his *Seminal Solid Light* series emerged. From these beginnings, McCall has continued to explore the potential of light as a sculptural medium.

Jim Campbell (opposite bottom)

Working from San Francisco, contemporary artist Jim Campbell specialises in LED light works such as *Scattered Light*, an installation that was ornamented in Madison Square Park Conservancy in 2010. Although he works primarily with light and electronics, Campbell also has experience as a filmmaker. Drawing upon this experience, Campbell produces multifaceted works that bring together divergent elements: film and sound, light and space. *Scattered Light* demonstrates this amalgamation as images of bodies pulse through the installation's lights in cinematic style. Through this installation, viewers are invited to consider how the two-dimensional performs within a three-dimensional space.

Brigitte Kowanz

Although she works with a wide array of materials—neon tubing, mirrors, text, aluminium and LED lights—Austrian artist Brigitte Kowanz's oeuvre is unified by one pursuit: the exploration of light. Kowanz began her work in the 1980s and has produced a diverse body of work comprising installations, settings and sculptures that derive from a robust range of inspiration. The beginning of her career is marked by an interest in how the world is suffused with light, evidenced by her colourful productions. Eventually, Kowanz's work transitioned into an examination of text and language. Language, it is implied, inevitably constructs our experiences of the world.

Doug Wheeler

Doug Wheeler's work experiments with ideas of perceptive experience. Wheeler is known as a pioneer of the 'light and space' movement popular during the 1960s and 1970s, which shaped his own practice. A versatile artist, Wheeler paints, draws, and produces installations; however, his fundamental interest in the play of space, volume and light draws together his various endeavours. Since his emergence as a young artist in southern California, Wheeler has continued to rework the conventions of light art.

Leo Villareal

New York based artist Leo Villareal is known for his groundbreaking LED compilations realised from complex algorithm based technology, placing him as a world leader in illumination art. His work references various twenty-first century art movements with some of his projects taking years from inception to completion. Villareal's public installations in the United States attract international interest. His 2013–2015 lighting installation for the San Francisco Oakland-Bay Bridge, *The Bay Lights*—consisting of 25,000 LED lights and costing $8 million—used the reflective properties of the water below to produce ripples of alluring sparkle, increasing the wonder of his composition.

Dan Flavin (above left)

American artist Dan Flavin's installations explore how light relates to colour and form, and even after his death in 1996 they continue to deliver a hothouse of perceptive possibilities. Flavin worked over several decades, and was inspired by the Minimalism and Op Art movements. The 1960s represented a change in direction for the artist when he developed his *Icons* series leading him to understand how electricity could be incorporated into his works. His outdoor installations with compositions of colour infused florescent light tubes delve into new artistic realms with the onset of night-time, as their transformative properties are unlocked and they become an instrument of sculpture.

Rafael Lozano-Hemmer (above right)

Award-winning electronic sound and light artist Mexican-Canadian Rafael Lozano-Hemmer is well known for his light and installation works. He completed a Bachelor of Science degree in Physical Chemistry at Concordia University in Montreal. His interest in architecture, technological theatre, and performance has inspired him to place emphasis on bringing people together and to consider impacts upon the community through his work. His large-scale connective work of light and sound, *Voice Tunnel*, in New York, reinforced this ethos. In this installation, the public was invited to speak into intercoms positioned throughout the tunnel where voice levels control light that scales the arched surfaces, and the louder the voice, the further light travels. The sound moved from one place towards the end of the tunnel as another intercom records, allowing for complete strangers to converse with one another.

Chris Levine

UK based artist Chris Levine uses and adapts his knowledge of laser technologies in his transformational, innovative art practice to create artwork. Levine sites his meditation practice as an inspiration whilst also embracing continual advancements in technology, working across multiple mediums and platforms including music, performance, installation, fashion, and design. He has created portraits of figures including Kate Moss and Grace Jones who are shown to have an ethereal glow with light seeping out from them. In 2004, Levine created an iconic portrait of Queen Elizabeth II in a meditative state—working continually to purify his interpretation until 'a level of stillness' was achieved.

Product Designers

Ingo Maurer (below)

Since the early 1960s, German industrial designer Ingo Maurer has developed lighting products and installations that question how we perceive light. His innovative work demonstrates how light plays with shadow to create elements of drama and surprise. Maurer's highly innovative and decorative Birdie Chandelier is made of tin-plated metal and either translucent or red cabling with goose-feathers attached to exposed halogen lamps. This creates the effect of fluttering winged birds taking flight upon adjacent walls in soft ghosting shadows.

Michael Anastassiades (right)

Cypriot minimalist product designer Michael Anastassiades founded his own design studio in London in 1994 after studying industrial design and engineering at the Royal College of Art in London. His kinetic lighting works master the relationship between art and design using modest materials. His ability to cleverly interpret the weightlessness of light has led him to create geometric and sculptural forms. Anastassiades' luminaires appear to be suspended in space delivering balance, functionalism and aestheticism at the end of a switch.

Paul Cocksedge (right)

Internationally acclaimed British-born Paul Cocksedge is admired for his pioneering work that uses the transformative power of materials in creating lighting works. His experiments with technology in order to challenge material constraints began in 2002 whilst studying at the Royal College of Art in London. His spherical, white Styrene light is composed of hundreds of heat-shrinked coffee cups from which light permeates through small portals creating a captivating array of dancing shadows on adjacent surfaces. The planetary dimension of this work considers Cocksedge's fascination with the fact that light is not bound by gravity.

Serge Mouille

Highly influential French goldsmith and industrial designer Serge Mouille was best known for his lighting fixtures. He learnt his craft after being admitted into the École des Arts Appliqués in Paris at age 13 to study metallurgy. Mouille's minimalist designs follow an ethos of simplicity as he considered other contemporary Italian designs to be too extravagant and complicated in their use of materials and colour. His Parisian flair is evident in the simplicity of his handmade lighting designs. Mouille's beautifully sculpted, enamelled white or black shades supported by slim metal rods utilise the natural expanse and reflection of light giving the onlooker the opportunity to touch and direct the light source for themselves.

Achille Castiglioni

Achille Castiglioni was one of the most important industrial designers of the twentieth century, renowned for his use of minimal materials for maximum effect. He initially studied architecture at the Politecnico di Milano, Italy and following Second World War, he and his brothers started up a design practice. They experimented with new materials that had been used by the defence industry producing iconic lights in the 1950s and 60s that are still under license today. In 1962, Castiglioni deemed his infamous Arco lamp—with an 8ft steel arm arching out of a white cararra marble rectangular base with chamfered corners—as his greatest design as it personified his unique style. His products, such as the Toio floor lamp, inspired by car reflectors conceived in the same year, continue to remain timeless with a fun and modern ethos.

Windfall (opposite top left)

Windfall, a crystal design practice based in Munich, run by Clarissa Dorn and Roel Haagmans, is renowned for their visionary ideas, passion and meticulous attention to detail. Their worldwide installations have redefined a new generation of contemporary crystal chandeliers and sculptural lamps. Windfall continually sets an exciting new benchmark in design as they incorporate the latest in both crystal and LED technology with each new collection.

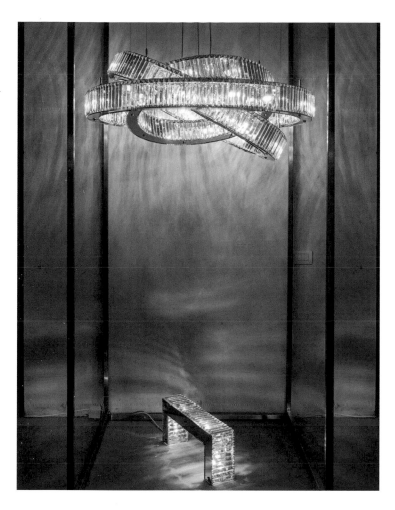

Tord Boontje

London-based Dutch product designer, Tord Boontje uses his understanding of historical artistry to create alluring pieces of lighting, glassware and furniture with a progressive twist. Boontje is inspired by nature, fairy tales, and the properties of light. Boontje's crystal Swarovski Blossom Chandelier was inspired by a romantic interpretation of nature allowing him to experiment and create a visual fairy tale. Boontje likes to work with the darkness that exists within the confines of an interior space in order to define his work. LED light sources are placed directly near the crystals to create a glistening manifestation of nature.

Poul Henningsen (below left)

Poul Henningsen was a Danish author, critic and one of the first lighting architects. He gained international fame and recognition for his sublime PH Artichoke Pendant, which was developed initially in 1958 for the Langelinie Pavillonen restaurant in Copenhagen, and is still recognised internationally for its geometric beauty in modern day culture. The PH Artichoke Pendant, manufactured by Louis Poulsen, emits diffused 360-degree glare free reflection. The 12-rod arches support 72 leaves guiding the light source away from the naked eye onto the descending leaves to give a uniquely soft light. In 2008, a fiftieth anniversary glass model complemented the range of white, copper and chrome finishes. Its popularity makes it one of the world's finest examples of incandescent luminaries and it is now produced with the option of using LED energy saving alternatives.

Philippe Starck

Multi award-winning French innovator and inventor Philippe Starck initially became known for his interior, product, industrial and architectural work in the 1980s. His fascination with materiality and how we relate to it began when he studied at the École Camondo in Paris. Starck has admitted that he is mostly 'elsewhere' with ideas conjured up in his dreams, often evolving into eclectic designs. His material products are infused with hidden social and cultural messages often involving politics, sex, poetry and comedy.

Tom Dixon (above right)

Tom Dixon, born in Tunisia and raised in London, began his career in the mid 1980s as a self-taught designer, welding furniture out of salvage materials. The anarchic punk movement of the 1980s enabled him to freely express his creative talents leading him to further his interest in the sustainability of materials and processes. In the late 1990s he became the creative director at Habitat and his interest in mid-twentieth century design flourished leading him to champion the return of classic designs back into the modern home. In 2003, Dixon achieved success with his highly reflective mirror ball light inspired by the space helmet. Dixon's evocative lighting collection is highly distinctive, and is often playful and sometimes quirky in style.

Architects

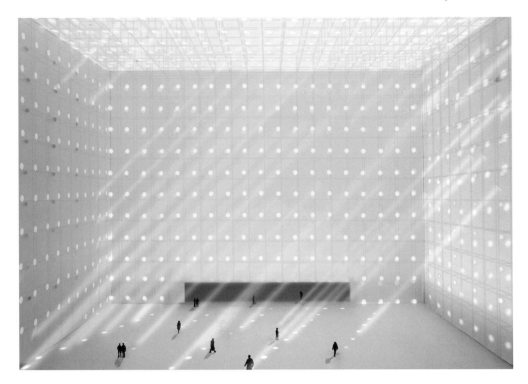

Le Corbusier

Swiss-French architect Le Corbusier's ability to convert his aptitude for design into stunning architecture secured his reputation as one of the pioneers of the modern architecture movement. His visionary approach and understanding of the democratic needs of a changing society—used together with evolving industrial design techniques—impacted his modernist style. He believed a house is 'a machine for living in'. His five points of architecture included the raising of the living space to a first floor level supported by pillars and leaving the internal space unencumbered by walls and other divisions. The importance of light formed the basis for much of his work, and the interplay of light with new modernistic materials, such as chrome and steel, became an inherent part of his design practice. His designs often include large panes of glass that invite natural light to flood into open interior spaces.

John Pawson (left)

British-born minimalist, John Pawson, travelled to Japan in his early twenties to further his understanding of the interrelationship between indoor and outdoor spaces. There, he observed architectural practices, and spent time in Shiro Kuramata's Tokyo studio. His visits to Kuramata's studio preceded his return to England, where he continued his exploration of architecture. Pawson began his career after studying at the Architectural Association School of Architecture in London. In 1981, he founded his own practice, which continues to operate today. The minimalist proposition of his works is assisted by both natural and artificial light. Pawson's ability to work with dense materials, using light to imbue mass with a sense of weightlessness, is awe-inspiring. He uses light to break tradition and to inform and guide his practice.

Alberto Campo Baeza (above and left)

Spanish-born minimalist architect Alberto Campo Baeza is fascinated with the concept of architecture as a 'built idea', stimulating his interest in the complicated relationships between gravity, light, space and time. In his 2013 award-winning work, the Pibamarmi Pavilion, he used light to reach the human psyche as he deployed it in juxtaposition with the heaviness of a suspended slab of travertine, evoking a sense of compression as visitors walked beneath it.

Tadao Ando (opposite bottom left)

Japanese architect Tadao Ando is renowned for his elegant yet simple architectural aesthetic, embodied in buildings such as his masterpiece The Church of the Light in the Osaka area, Japan. The church is meditative and emphasises simple concrete design over complex embellishment, allowing for the spiritual feel of the space to take precedence. Ando's work is influenced by Zen philosophies, and visitors find reprieve from outside strains of light inside the church. Light plays an important role in producing this tranquil, contemplative atmosphere. A striking feature of the church is its sunlit cruciform. In the morning, light from the east enters through the cruciform shape and illuminates the interior. Ando's speciality of utilising concrete to form glass-like surfaces enables light to define the chapel's character.

Frank Lloyd Wright (above)

The completion of Fallingwater, built 1936–1939, underpinned Frank Lloyd Wright's position as a visionary architect of the twentieth century. Fallingwater has been labelled as one of the best works of American architecture of all time, and follows his ideas of designing buildings that are in harmony with their environment. His belief that "form and function should be one" is expressively represented in his later work, the Solomon R. Guggenheim Museum in New York, built in 1959. Wright's idea was for visitors to ride the building's elevator to the top and work their way down to the atrium. The open rotunda design of the Solomon R. Guggenheim Museum allows for natural light to flood into the building and bounce off and around the white curvaceous levels.

Luis Barragán

Prizker Prize winner Luis Barragán set in motion modern Mexican architecture, inspired by the colourful palette of his homeland. He was influenced by his exploration of European Modernism and was deterred from the 'functionalism' of this style. He viewed space and architecture as vehicles to elicit an emotional response. His favoured themes—light and water—were used in creative conjunction with raw materials such as stone and wood. He believed that architecture should soothe the soul, and in his practice, he used creative applications of light to explore the properties of light, space and water.

Peter Zumthor

Swiss architect Peter Zumthor explores the interplay of light and atmosphere through his architectural practice. For Zumthor, the primary goal of architecture is to evoke an immediate reaction through the use of form. He believes that the metaphorical capacities of architecture are secondary to this objective, and his works foreground bodily perception in space and atmosphere. In his practice, Zumthor has been involved with many building projects that have shaped his view that atmosphere is affected by light. Thus, he believes that all buildings should emphasise atmosphere and seek to produce an emotional response from the viewer.

Renzo Piano

Italian architect Renzo Piano believes natural light is as much a part of the fabric of a building as the materials themselves. Piano's thought-provoking architecture spans five decades and ranges from the radical design of the Centre Georges Pompidou in Paris which he designed with Richard Rogers and Gianfranco Franchini in the 1970s, to the tallest European neo-futuristic skyscraper, The Shard in Southwark, London, inaugurated in 2012.

Piano's lighting artistry has been demonstrated many times, with his glass lantern roof structure design for the Harvard Art Museums' project winning him international acclaim. His mastery at drawing natural light into the architectural core of his buildings is well known.

Herzog & de Meuron (left)

Herzog & de Meuron are a Swiss architecture firm who have designed buildings around the world including their involvement with the Beijing National Stadium, designed for the 2008 Summer Olympics and Paralympics. Mirroring life on to the waters beside it, its crystalline jewel-like appearance has earned it the nickname, the 'Bird's Nest'. At night, its light-emitting properties give onlookers an imaginative prospect of what could be contained inside. The building's structure emulates the character of an athlete—strong, powerful and dynamic—and it is now currently used mostly for football games.

Oscar Niemeyer (below)

After participating in design projects in Brazil, Oscar Niemeyer gained the confidence to express his design aesthetic by using sculptural curves in the construction of concrete buildings. This propelled him into a new architectural philosophy, and gained him the reputation as a key figure of modern architecture. One of his greatest works, the Cathedral of Brasília, allows light to pervade through the flower-like crown of its hyperboloid structure. Supported by 16 curved columns composed of concrete, the colourful stained glass ceiling permits light to enter the building. The eye is drawn to these apertures towards the sky, while the presence of hanging angel sculptures illustrates the holistic qualities and spirituality of the internal religious space.

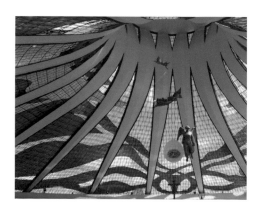

Buildings

Burj Khalifa, Dubai, UAE

In 2010, the Burj Khalifa hit the record books as the world's tallest architectural endeavour, standing at 829.8m. Towering over downtown Dubai, the jagged structure casts a needle-like shadow over the surrounding city. Elements of classic Islamic architecture, particularly seen in the approach to patterning, inform the design of the building. Daily sound and light shows pulsate light from over 6,600 incandescent fountain luminaries into jetted water shooting up to 150m high. This display of sound, light and colour is set on the Burj Khalifa Lake, to both native and international music, and can be viewed from up to 20 miles away. Within the building, built-in intelligence systems provide guestrooms, residences and commercial spaces with user-friendly interfaces that control varied artificial lighting needs.

Law Courts, Antwerp, Belgium

The Law Courts in Antwerp were conceptualised as a modern space, where architects Richard Rogers Partnership along with VK Studio, have moved away from the traditional, draconian designs of Antwerp. The strength of natural light has been utilised within the building to give a more open and lighter feel to the lower lying part of the building, which houses the heavy topic of law. Light was also a crucial concern in designing the dramatic pointed metal sails that form the roofline. These reflect the sun and incite the curiosity of a new visiting public. The architects for the Law Courts received the RIBA (Royal Institute of British Architects) European Award in 2007.

Yas Viceroy Hotel, Abu Dhabi, UAE (above)

The Yas Viceroy Hotel, built on the Formula One Yas Marina circuit in Abu Dhabi, echoes the excitement that Formula One racing elicits. Opened in 2009, it is the world's first hotel to extend over a Formula One circuit. It was designed to become an important landmark for the city as a modern hotel using local and international inspirations. The main feature of the building, the Grid Shell, a curvilinear 217m shell made of glass and steel, emits a constant spectacle of changing coloured lights through over 5,000 LED panels. So exuberant is this paragon of architecture that its warmth and glow can be seen from miles away as a glowing mist on the horizon.

National Centre for the Performing Arts, Beijing, China (left)

The National Centre for the Performing Arts, Beijing, also referred to as 'The Giant Egg' is an arts centre containing an opera house with a futuristic spacecraft-like aesthetic. In the conceptualisation of this building, French architect Paul Andreu considered light to be an essential part of the design aesthetic. He maximised the use of natural light, electing to use over 1,000 ultra-white sheets of glass due to their ability to transfer great amounts of light. During the day, the highly reflective titanium plates enveloping the eggshell exterior reflect onto the still waters of the adjacent man-made lake. Inside, the plates act as a beautiful brise soleil. Dynamic lighting at night gives this spectacular shape an optimistic, energising glow.

Markthal, Rotterdam, Holland

The functionalist, multipurpose Markthal building in Rotterdam provides an urban hub consisting of a market hall, commercial spaces and residential dwellings. Architecture practice MVRDV designed the building with an arched roof that contains 228 apartments above the public food markets. The arched ceiling of the building is covered with a colourful mural—10,000m^2— with enormous depictions of food, flowers and insects. Leading lighting systems provide daylight harvesting to save on energy. At night, dimming staircases function as directional guides and do not disturb the apartment residents' sleep. Design features such as these affirm the architects' understanding of how we react instinctively to light.

The Hepworth Wakefield, West Yorkshire, England

The Hepworth Wakefield is an art gallery named after British artist and sculptor Barbara Hepworth, and designed by British architect David Chipperfield. The gallery's design triumph was to optimise the use of natural lighting inside the gallery. Placement of slot lighting in the roof and the consideration of appropriate window sizing in the incongruous shaped framework have worked alongside a sophisticated daylight mapping system to control light in order to protect sensitive works. The design allows for views to the outside spaces including the garden and river, and it won the British Design Award in 2011.

ICEHOTEL, Jukkasjärvi, Sweden (above)
The ICEHOTEL in Jukkasjärvi, northern Sweden, is the world's first ice hotel and it has inspired others to attempt mastering snow form and ice design with vigour. Each year, designers from multidisciplinary backgrounds such as theatre, media production and interior design compete to get their sculptural endeavours accepted by a board of judges. Visitors, on the other hand, enjoy the sculptures in the hotel's glacial interior. With temperatures hovering at around -5°C it is a surreal experience. Carefully situated LED lights permeate the reflective interiors with colour, gesturing with shape and form, with some lights echoing the colours of the aurora borealis onto the icy constructs.

Sheikh Zayed Grand Mosque, Abu Dhabi, UAE (above right)
This visionary piece of contemporary architecture, first initiated by the late president of the United Arab Emirates (UAE), Sheikh Zayed bin Sultan Al Nahyan, magnificently articulates traditions from the Arab and Islamic World. Persian and Moorish architecture inspired the design with materials and artisans used from around the world. Its sheer opulence is evident in its materials including marble, semi-precious stones, gold and crystals. Lapis lazuli, red agate, amethyst and mother of pearl are worked into pillars, panels and hand-knotted carpets. Ceilings are ornamented with Swarovski crystals, and ornate, twinkling chandeliers adorn the hallways. The transformative qualities of light enhance this building's architectural magnificence, creating a spiritual dimension. The amount of luminescence is effortlessly altered to adhere to the waxing and waning of the moon.

Queen Elizabeth II Great Court, The British Museum, London, England (left)
The vast expanses of light within the Queen Elizabeth II Great Court are powerfully encountered as visitors journey into the heart of The British Museum. The glass roof—made up of tessellated windowpanes fitting into 6,100m²—acts as a huge sun canopy that one can see through to the sky beyond. In what is known as the largest covered space in Europe, visitors can view the old external architecture of the building, as it now forms the walls of the new internal Great Court space. This creative use of light within the Great Court allows for exploration from visitors in previously inaccessible areas, and this creation of new spaces has led to an overall connectivity of the museum space.

Guggenheim Museum Bilbao, Spain
Frank Gehry's Guggenheim Museum of modern and contemporary art is known as one of the most significant, innovative works of contemporary architecture. The 'Bilbao effect' refers to how the museum has transformed the city, yet it also denotes a negative connotation by some as the museum can be seen as a symbol of gentrification. The solid titanium, glass and limestone structure was intended by Gehry to show fluidity and movement as a reflection upon the surrounding Nervión river. Reflections that are naturally posted onto the water's surface examine the play of natural light on the man-made form through ever-changing levels of light, creating a flow of unique sensory experiences for the viewer.

Matrimandir, Auroville, India (below)
This symbolic building, otherwise known as the 'Temple of the Mother', is a place for concentration and revelation, and of significance for practitioners of integral yoga. Its mass and spherical shape signifies a deeper state of consciousness. A spherical crystal strategically sits within the ample sized Inner Chamber. Light is projected in a controlled way onto the crystal's centre via a heliostat, using natural sun rays to act as a 'searchlight'. Photoelectric sensors adjust the position of the sun's rays to ensure the accuracy of the point of light.

Natural Wonders

Northern Lights (right)

The aurora borealis, or northern lights as they are commonly known, are natural light displays caused by the interaction of the Earth's upper atmosphere with charged gas particles emitted at high speed out of the sun. Enthusiastic audiences from around the world travel to arctic regions within the northern hemisphere to observe the celestial spirit and phenomena of consistent rolling colours of green, blue, red and white dramatically orchestrated above the landscape to create a cinematic display. Named after the Roman goddess of dawn, the aurora borealis has for centuries been connected to mythical legends and faiths. It is referred to by the Sami, the indigenous people of Norway, as 'the light which can be heard'.

Glow-worms

Luminous yellow-green coloured glow-worms (members of the bioluminescent beetle family *Phengodidaie*) have the ability to convert 100 per cent of their energy input into light for practical uses of survival including attracting a mate, attracting prey and deterring predators. The chemical reaction that produces their bioluminescence comes from internal light organs. Glow-worms live in damp caves and riverbanks, and are seen all over the world in sparkling beads of colour. They are known for illuminating large, dark spaces such as subterranean caverns in New Zealand and Australia.

Antelope Canyon (left)

The upper and lower Antelope Canyon in Page, Arizona, in America's south-west are a result of flash flooding that carved out the inner space of the canyon providing passages and slots for natural light to shine through. These passages and light slots epitomise how light transforms the way that we see space and what we derive from it. The canyon sits on the reservation of the native Navajo tribes, and is said to be of spiritual significance—images of birds, eagles, faces and other forms are said to appear within the smooth, wave-like sandstone walls. Sunlight funnels down into the cavities past the incongruously shaped overhangs, enabling different intensities of light to reach hidden pockets, and enhancing the rippling effect on the terracotta coloured walls to give a sense of magical stillness.

Bioluminescent Plankton

Bioluminescent plankton, also known as sea sparkle, is an extraordinary spectacle of bright neon light caused by chemicals released by tiny organisms due to the sensation of moving waves combined with oxygen. The existence of this blue luminescence follows a circadian rhythm teasing the onlooker into realms of other-worldliness. The glowing swathes of blue light become a focus of visual wonderment whilst set against a night landscape.

The Marble Caves of Patagonia (below)

At the southernmost tip of Chile, the Marble Caves residing within the General Carrera Lake provide a display of how the beauty of natural sculpture is enhanced through the dynamic levels of natural light. These miraculous monuments of glacial silt in rich turquoises and indigo blues were formed over 6,000 years ago. They stretch into cavernous reaches and seduce the water's surface by giving a diffused reflectance with a brightness that leaves the viewer with a sense of wonderment.

Hornsund Fjord Glacier (left)

In Svalbard, Norway, light permeates through the quartz structure of a glacier in the Hornsund fjord, acting as a spyhole with an outlook towards the naturally carved and sculptured mountains and valleys—the work of winter over many generations. Svalbard is the northernmost inhabited region of Europe, and possesses 18 magnificent glaciers, the largest of Norway's icy forms. Daylight enhances the beauty of the glacier's crystalline structure with reflections that bounce off the snow cover making the landmass appear larger in the glistening fjord waters.

Blue Hour (below)

The human fascination with the sensory eminence that sunrise and sunset imbues, owes its reputation in part to the power of the Blue Hour. In the relatively short phase of the twilight period, when the sun rises and descends over the earth's sphere, a pure blue hue is seen caused by indirect light emitted from the sun. The purity of the blue light can confuse the spectator into thinking that it may be conversely the beginning or the end to the day. This twilight period also continually inspires artists.

Moonbow

A moonbow is created when the moon is at a low position of a maximum of 42-degrees from the horizon allowing for light to be reflected off its own surface, refracting off atmospheric vapours or droplets in the air rather than through the effects of direct sunlight upon it. Seen in many countries, spray moonbows are the result of fog or mist with waterfalls exemplifying their beauty. Colours of the moonbow often appear white to the naked eye, but are unmasked by long photographic exposures. They are also sometimes encased in a white halo.

Uluru/Ayers Rock (above)

Uluru, or Ayers Rock as it is also known, is a large sandstone rock formation, listed as a UNESCO World Heritage site and part of the Kata Tjuta National Park in Australia. It is a sacred site to the native Aboriginal people, and celebrated for the play of light at sunrise and sunset with its distinctive changes in rich red colouration. Lightning emanating from a purple thunderous sky sends flashes of light containing millions of volts of electricity—forking light in jagged and asymmetrical forms—against the magnificent backdrop of the darkened sky and arid desert landscape. Located near the centre of Australia, the rock rises 348m out of the desert plain with a massive surface area of 9.4km.

Fireflies

Fireflies, also known as lightning bugs, are insects that use bioluminescence light emissions during twilight to attract mates or prey. It is believed that in the sixteenth century, Baroque painter Caravaggio used the powder of dried fireflies on canvases to create a photosensitive surface on which he projected the image he was to paint. More recently, scientists have mimicked the way fireflies produce bioluminescence through their tiny scales, and have applied a similar method to LED lighting wafers, improving the efficiency of LED lighting by over 55 per cent.

The Power House

Glossary

Absorption
An amount of light absorbed by an object, instead of being reflected. Matt surfaces and woollen fabrics are least likely to reflect light.

Accent Lighting
Lighting directed onto a particular object to focus attention onto it.

Ambient Lighting
A soft, indirect light that fills the whole of the space, often creating a warm glow in the room.

Aperture
An opening through which light travels such as a window or wall opening.

Artificial Light
Illumination produced by electrical processes.

Backlighting
The process of illuminating the subject from the back. The lighting instrument and the viewer face each other, with the subject in between.

Ballast
A control device that regulates the current to lamps and provides sufficient voltage to start lamps.

Beam Angle, Width or Spread
A measure of the spread of light produced by a lamp or luminaire.

Binning
The way of measuring an LED's colour and the tolerances allowed in which to deliver it to market.

Biodynamic Lighting Systems
Intelligent systems that mimic daylight creating shifts in output and colour temperature according to the time of day.

Black Mirror Effect
When little or no natural daylight exists, one's own reflection is seen when looking through glass.

Brightness
An attribute of visual perception in which a source appears to be radiating or reflecting light.

Brise Soleils
A structural feature that deflects sunlight and reduces the effects of light emanating from the sun.

Cable Voltage Drop
A reduction in electrical pressure in a cable resulting from increasing distance from the power source or increased power (wattage or current) drawn along the cable.

Candela (cd)
A common candle emits light with a luminous intensity of roughly one candela. It is the unit of measurement of luminous intensity of a light source in a given direction.

Candle Power
Luminous intensity expressed in candelas.

Coffer
An architectural sunken panel, usually square or rectangular to mirror the shape of a room.

Colour-corrected
The addition of phosphors in a lamp to create better colour rendering.

Colour Quality Scale (CQS)
A method of accurately measuring how the colour of surfaces appears using a standard number of 15 colour samples.

Colour Rendering Index (CRI)
A quantitative measure of the ability of a light source to reveal the colours of various objects faithfully in comparison with an ideal or natural light source.

Construction Drawing
A graphic representation of the work to be done in the construction of a project that supplements specifications.

Cornice Lighting
Lighting from sources that are shielded by a panel parallel to the wall and attached to the ceiling or to the upper edge of the wall and which distribute light over the wall.

Correlated Colour Temperature (CCT)
A specification of the colour appearance of the light emitted by a lamp, relating its colour to the colour of light from a reference source when heated to a particular temperature, measured in degrees Kelvin (K).

Cove Lighting
Cove lighting is a form of indirect lighting built into ledges, recesses or valences in a ceiling or high on the walls of a room. It directs light up towards the ceiling and down adjacent walls.

Cowl
An accessory used to reduce the glare from a light fitting.

Cross Lighting
A technique to illuminate a subject such as a tree or sculptural object from two or more sides to reveal the three-dimensional form in a striking perspective.

Digital Addressable Lighting Interface (DALI)
A data protocol which was developed by multiple manufacturers to ensure compatibility and interchangeability between control and light fixtures.

Daylight
The combination of light from the sky and sunlight.

Daylight Harvesting
A way to use daylight to offset the amount of electric lighting needed to properly light a space in order to reduce energy consumption.

Daylighting
Daylighting is the practice of placing windows or other openings and reflective surfaces so that during the day natural light provides effective internal lighting.

Daylight Sensors
A device that measures ambient light levels used to help control lighting levels and conserve energy.

Decorative Lighting
Lighting used to attract attention that is aesthetically pleasing.

Diffused Lighting
A general illumination that appears to come from multiple directions.

Diffuser
A shielding device designed to sit over a luminaire to spread light in more than one direction.

Digital Multiplex (DMX)
A system to control, dim or programme colour.

Dimmer
Dimmers are devices used to lower the brightness of a light. By changing the voltage waveform applied to the lamp, it is possible to lower the intensity of the light output.

Dimmer Switches
A device to facilitate a change in lighting levels.

Direct Glare
Where there is glare resulting from high luminance in the visual environment that is directly visible.

Disability Glare
Glare that reduces the ability to perceive the visual information needed for a particular activity.

Downlight
A luminaire that is used to project light onto an object or feature below.

Driver
An electronic power supply required to power an LED source.

Edge Lighting
Illumination of a material by running a light source along its edge.

Efficacy
The way in which the efficiency of a light source is measured.

Electrical Legend
A key of electrical symbols for a plan.

End-emitting Fibre-Optic Lighting System
Often used for star lighting, it gives an end glow to the end of each of the cylindrical optic fibres.

Fade Rate
The rate at which light levels decrease.

Fibre-Optic Lighting
A system of projecting light along a number of optical glass fibres.

Filter
A glass or metal accessory that alters the characteristics of light beam patterns. It can affect the colour or shape.

Fish Tape
A device used to pull wires through tight spaces or conduit.

Fluorescence
Fluorescence is the emission of light by a substance that has absorbed light or other electromagnetic radiation.

Fluorescent Lamp
A fluorescent lamp or tube is a low pressure discharge lamp that uses an electric current which excites the mercury vapour and causes the phosphor coating on the inside of the bulb to glow.

Foot Candle (fc)
The unit measurement of light that falls upon a surface within a one foot radius.

Framing Projector
A luminaire that can be adjusted to precisely frame an object with light.

Ganging
The grouping of two or more controls in one enclosure.

Grazing
When a light source is set at a low angle to the object that is being lit. This creates dramatic shadows.

Halogen
An incandescent lamp containing halogen gas—it is whiter and more brilliant in appearance than traditional bulbs.

Hardwire
A method of luminaire installation using a junction box.

Heat Sink
A passive device used to dissipate heat away from an LED.

High-Intensity Discharge (HID) Lamp
A category of lamp that emits light through an electricity activating pressurised gas in a bulb. They are bright and energy efficient light sources used mainly in exterior environments.

Honeycomb Lens
A lens which is added as an accessory to light fittings that has a honeycomb shaped grid used to reduce glare.

Illuminance (E)
Illuminance is light falling on a surface measured in foot candles (fc) or lux (lx).

Incandescent Lamp
An electric light that produces light with a wire filament heated to a high temperature by an electric current passing through it until it glows.

Infinity Lighting
Creates the illusion of depth within an architectural detail.

Infrared (IR)
A wave of light that is in the area beyond the visible part of the colour spectrum—the light that is at the far edge of the red hue of a rainbow that we cannot detect with the naked eye. It is used for many applications including TV controls and infrared cameras.

Integrated Emergency Battery Packs
These devices require a dedicated power supply. They remain fully charged so that they operate through battery life when power is cut in an emergency.

Junction Box
An enclosure for joining wires behind walls and ceilings.

Key
Also known as a legend. Annotates all symbols on a plan.

Kinetic Lighting
The energy emitted through the movement of a light source.

Lamp
The lighting industry name for a light bulb.

Lamp Life
The expected life of a lamp in operating hours based on laboratory tests. This can vary enormously depending on the exact conditions in which it operates.

Layering Light
The use of a combination of luminaires placed at different heights to create a cohesive scheme.

Light Pipes
Also known as light tubes, they are a method for transporting or distributing natural light often to spaces where there is none.

Light Sheet
A slim profiled LED backlighting unit which delivers even illumination used to create a dramatic wall of light or to illuminate surface materials such as decorative glass and graphics.

Light Shelf
A light shelf is a horizontal surface that reflects daylight deep into a building. Light shelves are placed above eye level and have high reflectance upper surfaces, which reflect daylight onto the ceiling and deeper into the space.

Light Slot
Light slots are linear cuts mounted into or upon the architectural framework.

Light Emitting Diodes (LEDs)
A semiconductor device that emits light when an electric current is passed through it. Described as solid-state lighting, which distinguishes the technology from other lamps such as filament or gas discharge.

Light Fittings Legend
A key of all light fittings for a plan.

Lighting Plan
An outline illustrating where light fittings are to be placed and how they are to be circuited and controlled.

Lighting Schedule
Provides and keeps track of information about all electrical equipment used for a given lighting scheme.

Lighting Control System
An intelligent network based lighting control solution that incorporates communication between various systems.

Line voltage
The number of volts in a household current that is particular to each country.

Louver / Louvre
A slatted device attached as an accessory to a light fitting to reduce glare.

Low Voltage Lighting
Typically 12 or 24 volts. A transformer is used to help convert the voltage to a lower level.

Lumen (lm)
A measure of the total amount of visible light emitted by a source. Lumens are related to lux in that one lux is one lumen per m^2.

Lumen Per Watt (lm/W)
The standard measure for comparing the efficiency of light bulbs or lamps to see which produces more light for less power.

Luminaire
An essential tool for controlling light sources and consists of ballasts/power supplies; reflectors; shielding/diffusion components and housings.

Luminaire Efficiency
The percentage of light produced by the light source that is then emitted by the luminaire.

Luminance (L)
Luminance is a photometric measure of the luminous intensity per unit area of light travelling in a given direction. It describes the amount of light that passes through, is emitted or reflected from a particular area, and falls within a given solid angle.

Luminance Flux (F)
Luminance flux is the measure of the perceived power of light, adjusted to reflect the varying sensitivity of the human eye to different wavelengths of light.

Lux (lx)
The standard international unit of illuminance, or luminance flux incident on a unit area, frequently defined as one lumen per square metre (lm/m^2).

Momentary Button Dimming
A touch button dimming system that requires remote dimming packs. The major feature includes allowing artificial light to be dimmed from multiple locations.

Moonlighter
A light fitting that simulates the effect of moonlighting. Often used in gardens and courtyards, a fitting is set high up on a tree to light down through its branches creating dappled patterns of light.

Motion Sensor
Working as a component of a system that automatically performs a task when alerted by movement within an area.

Neon Lighting
A source of light often used as signage in the shape of letters, signs or shapes. It is made out of a tubular glass framework that is filled with neon gas and phosphors.

Occupancy Sensor (Vacancy Sensor)
A lighting control device that detects occupancy of a space by people and turns the lights on or off automatically, using infrared, ultrasonic or microwave technology.

Op Art Movement
Also known as optical art—a style of visual art that uses optical illusions, usually seen in black and white patterns giving the impression of movement.

Organic Light-Emitting Diodes (OLEDs)
Organic light-emitting diodes (OLEDs) are based on organic (carbon based) materials. In contrast to LEDs, which are small point sources, OLEDs are made in sheets that provide a diffuse area light source.

Phosphors
A substance that exhibits the phenomenon of luminescence. Phosphors are coated on to LEDs to alter the colour of light emitted.

Photocells
Allow lighting circuits to provide artificial light from dusk and for a fixed time period. Also known as Daylight Sensors.

Photosensor
A control device that activates luminaires subject to lighting levels within the space.

PIR (Passive Infra-Red Motion Sensor)
An electronic sensor that measures infrared (IR) light within its field of sight.

Polymer Light Emitting Diodes (PLEDs)
An emissive technology, as light is emitted as a function of its electrical operation they are used predominantly for full spectrum colour displays.

Reflectance
The ratio of the amount of light reflected from a surface to the illuminance falling upon it.

Reflected Ceiling Plan (RCP)
The plan of a ceiling projected onto a flat plane directly below, which shows the size and location of light fixtures and other objects within the ceiling.

Reflector
A device for controlling the beam of light emitted from a lamp.

Rotary Dimmers
Allows light to be dimmed from one location, as well as having a minimum and maximum load per circuit.

Sconce
A wall-mounted decorative light.

Seasonal Affective Disorder (SAD)
A type of depression that has a seasonal pattern. The episodes of depression tend to occur at the same time each year, usually during the winter.

Silhouetting
Allows for dramatic lighting effects that emphasise two-dimensional forms of three-dimensional works.

Solid-State Lighting (SSL)
This refers to a type of lighting that uses semiconductor light-emitting diodes (LEDs), organic light-emitting diodes (OLEDs), or polymer light-emitting diodes (PLEDs).

Sparkle Wheel
A metal disc with apertures to allow a random sequence of light to pass through.

Spotlighting
An effective way to add drama and impact to specific artwork or decorative accessories. Directional spotlights allow for precise control over which areas are lit.

Spread Lens
A glass lens used to diffuse and widen, or elongate light beam patterns.

Task Lighting
Lighting that is designed to give the work surface the most appropriate level of light.

Track Lighting
Light source emanating from an electrified metal channel.

Transformer
A magnetic or electronic device, which increases or decreases the voltage.

Tungsten
Incandescent lighting using a bulb with a filament made of the metal tungsten.

Ultraviolet light (UV)
A form of radiation that is not visible to the human eye. It is in an invisible part of the electromagnetic spectrum given off by a light source, a crackling fire and stars.

UV (Ultraviolet light) Filter
A coating or lens that prevents the harmful emissions of ultra-violet light from artificial light sources.

Voltage Drop
The decrease in voltage between the fitting and the driver resulting in a loss of power and light output.

Volts (v)
Measure the pressure, or force, of electricity.

Watt (W)
A measurement of power, used to describe the power consumed by a light source.

Societies and Bodies

Europe

ALD
Association of Lighting Designers
www.ald.org.uk

BIID
British Institute of Interior Design
www.biid.org.uk

CEDIA
Custom Electronic Design & Installation
Association
www.cedia.org

CIBSE
The Chartered Institution of Building
Services Engineers
www.cibse.org

CIE
The International Commission on Illumination
www.cie.co.at

CLD
Certified Lighting Designer
www.cld.global

IALD
International Association of Lighting
Designers Professionals
www.iald.org

IDA
International Dark-Sky Association
www.darksky.org

IIDA
International Interior Design Association
www.iida.org

ILP
Institute of Lighting Professionals
www.theilp.org.uk

LCA
Lighting Controls Association
www.lightingcontrolsassociation.org

LET
Lighting Education Trust
www.lightingeducationtrust.org

LFP
Lighting For People
www.lightingforpeople.eu

LIA
Lighting Industry Association
www.thelia.org.uk

PLDC
Professional Lighting Design Convention
www.pld-c.com

RIBA
Royal Institute of British Architects
www.architecture.com/

SBID
Society of British and International Design
www.sbid.org

SLL
Society of Light and Lighting
www.cibse.org/society-of-light-and-lighting-sll

UK Green Building Council
www.ukgbc.org

North America

AIA
The American Institute of Architects
www.aia.org

ALA
American Lighting Association
www.americanlightingassoc.com

ASID
American Society of Interior Designers
www.asid.org

IES
Iluminating Engineering Society of North
America
www.ies.org

IIDA
International Interior Design Association
www.iida.org

NAED
National Association of Electrical
Distributors
www.naed.org

NAILD
National Association of Independent
Lighting Distributors
www.naild.org

NEMA
National Electrical Manufacturers
Association
www.nema.org

USGBC
US Green Building Council
www.usgbc.org

Image Credits

Alan Higgs Architects
www.alanhiggsarchitects.com
Photographer: Peter Cook
www.petercookphoto.com
pp 36–37, 108, 109, 110, 111, 112, 113, 114, 115
Photographer: Leonardo Fiorini
www.leonardofiorini.com
pp 116–117, 118, 119, 120–121

Alberto Campo Baeza
Photographer: Giovanni de Sandre
p 174

Antelope Canyon. Lucas Löffler,
The Antelope Canyon in Arizona, 2006. Image
sourced from Wikimedia Commons, license:
public domain
p 178

Anthony McCall, *Between You and I*, 2006.
Installation view at Peer/The Round Chapel,
London, 2006
Photographer: Hugo Glendinning
p 170

BBF Fielding Architecture Ltd.
www.bbf-fielding.co.uk
Photographer: Light IQ
www.lightiq.com
pp 40, 41

Blue Hour. *The mining lamp (30 meters
high, made by Otto Piene) on the Halde
Rheinpreußen (Moers, North-Rhine Westfalia,
Germany) during the blue hour, on the right the
sunset*, 2010. Image sourced from Wikimedia
Commons, license: CC BY-SA 3.0 DE
p 179

C.W. Eisner, Inc.,
www.cweisner.com
Photographer: Laura Kelly
pp 47 bottom, 59, 60, 62, 63, 69, 71, 86, 87,
102–103, 134–135, 136–137, 138, 139
Photographer: Light IQ, www.lightiq.com
pp 47 top right, 58

Carden Cunietti
www.carden-cunietti.com
Photographer: Light IQ
www.lightiq.com
pp 180–181

Carlos Cruz-Diez, *Chromosaturation*,
2010, at the exhibition Suprasensorial:
Experiments in Light, Color, and Space,
The Museum of Contemporary Art (MOCA),
Los Angeles. © Carlos Cruz-Diez / Adagp,
Paris, 2015
p 170

Charlotte Rowe Garden Design
www.charlotterowe.com
Photographer: Light IQ
www.lightiq.com
pp 140–141, 146, 147, 148, 149, 152 top,
153, 154, 156, 157, 158, 159, 162, 164, 165

Christa Luntzel
Photographer: Rob Cadman
www.viewcamera.co.uk
p 56
Photographer: Light IQ
www.lightiq.com
p 57

Clive Sall Architecture Ltd.
www.clivesallarchitecture.com
Photographer: Laura Kelly
p 33

Cloud Design Studios Ltd.
www.cloudstudios.co.uk
Photographer: Andrew Beasley
www.abeasley.com
pp 84, 85

Culture Creative
www.culturecreative.co.uk
p 167

Dan Flavin. *Dan Flavin, Structure and clarity,
Tate Modern Museum, London*, 2014. Image
sourced from Wikimedia Commons, license:
CC BY 2.0
p 171

David Long Architects
www.dlaltd.com
Photographer: Michele Panzeri,
www.panzeri.co.uk
pp 21, 38, 39, 76, 77

Frank Lloyd Wright. Lisa Bettany,
Guggenheim, NYC fisheye, 2012. Image
sourced from Flickr, license: CC BY-SA 2.0
p 175

Gardenmakers Garden Design
www.garden-makers.co.uk
Photographer: Light IQ
www.lightiq.com
pp 160, 161

Guy Hollaway Architects
www.guyhollaway.co.uk
Photographer: Paul Freeman
www.prwfreeman.co.uk
pp 144, 145

Herzog & de Meuron. *Beijing national
stadium; Architect: Herzog & de Meuron,
ArupSport, China Architectural Design &
Research Group*, 2011. Image sourced from
Wikimedia Commons, license: CC BY 2.5
p 175

Hornsund Fjord glacier © Paul Nicklen/
National Geographic Creative
p 179

ICEHOTEL. *Ice Hotel Church @
Jukkasjärvi*, 2007. Image sourced from
Flickr, license: CC BY 2.0
p 177

Ingo Maurer, Birdie (Pendant Lamp), 2002.
Metal, 12 low-voltage bulbs, goose-feather
wings. 100cm x 70cm © Ingo Maurer
GmbH
p 172

Jim Campbell, *Scattered Light*, 2010. Temporary Public Project Commissioned by the Madison Square Park Conservancy. Madison Square Art, New York. Custom electronics, LEDs, light bulbs, wire, steel. 200cm x 50cm x 40cm. Image courtesy of the Madison Square Park Conservancy
Photographer: James Ewing
p 171

John Pawson
Photographer: Gilbert McCarragher
p 174

Johnny Grey Studios
www.johnnygrey.com
p 94
Photographer: Glenn Dearing
www.glenndearing.com
pp 124–125 126, 127, 128, 129, 130–131, 132, 133
Photographer: Jake Fitzjones
www.jakefitzjones.com
pp 88, 89, 90, 91, 98, 99, 100, 101

Kay Pilsbury Thomas Architects
www.kpt.co.uk
Photographer: Light IQ
www.lightiq.com
pp 18, 19

Kevin Murphy Garden Design
www.kevinmurphy.co.uk
Photographer: Laura Kelly
pp 142 right, 150–151, 152 bottom

Laura Kelly Photography
pp 24, 25, 52, 53

Leonardo Fiorini Photography
www.leonardofiorini.com
pp 74, 75

LifeHouse
www.lifehouseuk.com
p 80
Photographer: Light IQ
www.lightiq.com

Light IQ, photography
www.lightiq.com
pp 26–27, 155, 163, 166

Light IQ, plans
www.lightiq.com
pp 92, 93, 94, 95, 96, 97

Matrimandir, Auroville.
Image courtesy of Auroville Outreach Media
p 177

Maurizio Pellizzoni
www.mpdlondon.co.uk
Photographer: Jake Fitzjones
www.jakefitzjones.com
pp 78–79

Melanie J Canaway
Photographer: Leonardo Fiorini
www.leonardofiorini.com
pp 34, 68

Michael Anastassiades, Mobile Chandelier 1, 2008. Black patinated brass, mouth blown opaline spheres. Pendant rod length to order
p 172

National Theatre for the Performing Arts, Beijing. *The Egg*, 2010. Image sourced from Wikimedia Commons, license: CC BY-SA 3.0
p 176

Northern Lights. Diana Robinson, *Northern Lights over Reykjanes Peninsula Sea Stacks, Iceland*, 2015. Image sourced from Flickr, license: CC BY-ND 2.0
pp 168–169

Northern Lights. Diana Robinson, *Northern Lights over the Reykjanesviti Lighthouse, Reykjanes Peninsula, Iceland*, 2015. Image sourced from Flickr, license: CC BY-ND 2.0
p 178

Olafur Eliasson, *Notion Motion*, 2005. HMI lamps, tripods, water, foil, projection foil, wood, nylon, sponge, stainless steel, motor. Image courtesy of Studio Olafur Eliasson
p 170

Oscar Niemeyer. *Interior da Catedral Metropolitana de Brasília*, 2013. Image sourced from Wikimedia Commons, license: CC BY-SA 3.0
p 170

Panorama Property Development Ltd.
www.ppdltd.co.uk
Photographer: Colin Gates
www.cgpdesign.com
pp 12–15, 48–49, 50, 61, 65

Paul Cocksedge. Styrene, 2005
www.paulcocksedgestudio.com
Photographer: Richard Brine
p 172

Peter Leonard
Photographer: Richard Bryant
www.richardbryant.co.uk
pp 1, 4–5, 42, 43, 64, 72, 73, 83

Poul Henningsen and Louis Poulsen, PH Snowball. Image courtesy of Louis Poulsen A/S
p 173

Powell Tuck Associates
www.powelltuckassociates.co.uk
Christa Luntzel, Interior Design
Photographer: Rob Cadman
www.viewcamera.co.uk
p 28

Powell Tuck Associates
www.powelltuckassociates.co.uk
Photographer: Rob Cadman
www.viewcamera.co.uk
pp 16–17
Photographer: Light IQ
www.lightiq.com
pp 20, 22
Nathalie Priem Photography
www.nathaliepriem.com
p 23

Queen Elizabeth II Great Court, The British Museum. Andrew Stawarz, *The Great Court*, 2010. Image sourced from Flickr, license: CC BY-ND 2.0
p 177

Rafael Lozano-Hemmer, *Voice Tunnel, Relational Architecture 21*, 2013. Commissioned by: Park Avenue Tunnel, NYC DOT "Summer Streets"
Photographer: James Ewing
p 171

Rhino Rock LLP
www.rhinorock.co.uk
Photographer: Leonardo Fiorini
www.leonardofiorini.com
p 143

Sebastian Rogers
Photographer: Light IQ
www.lightiq.com
pp 46, 142

Sheikh Zayed Grand Mosque Center. Hisham Binsuwaif, *Sheikh Zayed Grand Mosque*, 2012. Image sourced from Flickr, license: CC BY-SA 2.0
p 177

Simon Brown Interiors
www.simonbrowninteriors.com
Photographer: Light IQ
www.lightiq.com
p 81

Studio Indigo
www.studioindigo.co.uk
Photographer: James Balston
www.jamesbalston.com
pp 6, 9, 10, 11, 29
Photographer: Light IQ
www.lightiq.com
p 8

Sutton Griffin Architects
www.suttongriffin.co.uk
pp 122, 123

Tadao Ando, Church of the Light. Image courtesy of Tadao Ando Architect & Associates.
Photographer: Mitsuo Matsuoka
pp 175

Taylor Howes Designs
www.taylorhowes.co.uk
Photographer: Laura Kelly
pp 30, 31, 44, 45, 82
Photographer: Leonardo Fiorini
www.leonardofiorini.com
pp 104, 105, 106, 107
Photographer: Light IQ
www.lightiq.com
pp 54, 55

The Marble Caves of Patagonia. Javier Vieras, *Marble cathedral inside*, 2013. Image sourced from Flickr, license: CC BY 2.0
p 179

Tom Dixon. *Tom Dixon: Mirror Ball Pendant Lights*. Image sourced from Wikimedia Commons, license: CC BY-SA 3.0
p 173

Uluru / Ayers Rock. *Scenic ayers rock, Uluru national park, Northern territory, Australia*, 2008. Image sourced from Picasa, license: CC BY-SA 3.0
p 179

Windfall, Contemporary Crystal Lighting
www.windfall-gmbh.com
p 173

Yas Viceroy Hotel, Abu Dhabi. Rob Atler, *The Yas Hotel – Yas Marina Circuit*, 2011. Image sourced from Flickr, license: CC BY 2.0
p 176

All images that are sourced from Wikimedia Commons, Flickr and Picasa are published under Creative Commons Licenses found at: http://creativecommons.org/licenses/

Acknowledgements

My thanks go firstly to Philip, my brother, who has successfully managed Light IQ (and me) for 15 years—we would never have travelled so far without you. Ally, who has allowed me to realise the book and kept the momentum. Gerardo, who as Design Director takes the team to greater heights. Sally, the inspiration and Honor, who led me to her. Uncle John, our first logo. Simone and Kelvin, for love, curries and worldly advice. Izzy, Lynda, Agnieszka, Natalie, Jackie, Laura, Althea, Adam, Kirstie, Tongqing, Roberto, Alessandra, Jay, Rafaela, Vanessa, Ros, Natasha HD, Abby and Peter, Natasha RD, Tom, Simon, Matt, Rishi, Sandra, Megan, Kane, Moni, Note, Victoria, Tomas, Leeling, Gemma, Kabir, Alex, Josh, Prasit, Charlotte, Rebecca C, Robert, Nabil, Ireneusz, Omer, Ellie and Ella, whose friendship, support and inspiration I have always cherished.

Mercy, for ensuring our home is peaceful and happy.

The incredibly talented interior designers, architects and landscapers who I continue to learn from. Their dedication to detail and the clients is second to none. Robert Taussig, who encouraged Light IQ. Significant individuals, whose loyalty and support allowed Light IQ to mature from the beginning: Diana McKnight, Jenny Gibbs, Marcy Brown, Tarquin Gorst, David Ambrose, Riki Shasha, Ngila Boyd, Mike Fisher, Arne Maynard, Charlotte Rowe, Simon Brown, Alasdair Cameron, Iain Macdonald, Juliette Byrne, Stephen Woodhams, Adrienne Chinn, James Agace, Gail Taylor, Karen Howes, Jane Landino, Guy Hollaway, Adrian Lees, Christa Luntzel, Nicola and Gemma Dudgeon, Peter Leonard, Tim and Rupert, Nick Yeates, Johnny Grey, Alan Higgs, Susan Crewe, Maurizio Pellizzoni, Gerri Gallagher, Louise Holt, Naomi Pound, Kate Slesinger, Iain Johnson and Mark Ridler. Your support has been invaluable.

The incredible photographers who have made this book possible, whose task to master and capture the invisible medium—thank you.

Light IQ's clients, who unanimously wish to remain confidential—thank you—none of it would be possible without you. In realising your dreams, I have found mine.

My mother always said: 'the world is your oyster'; for your love, belief, strength and support—thank you. My father for providing the love and moral compass through which we travel—you remain my inspiration.

My siblings for their friendship and laughter, and to Granny Tai Tai who kept us all together.

Lastly, to the greatest support team on earth, my incredible husband, Andrew and beautiful children, Zach and Honor—for their unfailing love.

—

Rebecca Weir

Having taken this unchartered journey into light I have Rebecca to thank for my deepening knowledge of this endlessly fascinating subject, and for all the fun we've had in conceptualising the book.

I am forever grateful to those who have encouraged me, my dear friends particularly Anne-Marie and Carol whose faith in me has been unstinting and to my much loved family— my kind and caring husband, my son who has given me the impetus to work so hard and to my Uncle John and sister Jo, for their unwavering love and support. And for those who came before—my loving grandparents, my beautiful mother and my darling dog, Bess who I lost along the way. I know I have much to be thankful for.

—

Allyson Coates

Colophon

Artifice books on architecture
10A Acton Street
London
WC1X 9NG

t. +44 (0)207 713 5097
f. +44 (0)207 713 8682
sales@artificebooksonline.com
www.artificebooksonline.com

All opinions expressed within this publication are those of the authors
and not necessarily of the publisher.

Designed by Matthew Boxall at Artifice books on architecture.

British Library Cataloguing-in-Publication Data.
A CIP record for this book is available from the British Library.

ISBN 978 1 908967 71 8

Artifice books on architecture is an environmentally responsible
company. *The Languages of Light: A Creative Approach to Residential
Lighting* is printed on sustainably sourced paper.